The Overconfidence Instinct

Why Winning Convinces You You're Better Than You Are

Jordan Ellis

First edition, 2026

Published by Jordan Ellis

Contents

Contents

Foreword

I started collecting these stories because I kept noticing an odd asymmetry in how people talked about money. Ask about a loss and you'll get a paragraph — bad timing, a thing nobody could have seen coming. Ask about a win and you'll get a sentence, flat, like a fact of nature: *I have a good eye for this.* Nobody ever needed three paragraphs to explain why they were right. Only why they were wrong.

That asymmetry sat with me longer than I expected it to. I've watched a man triple a small account on a handful of lucky calls and start describing himself as someone who "understands the market better than most people." I've watched a woman turn one well-timed business decision into a personal legend she repeated at dinner parties for a decade, embellished a little more each retelling. I've watched both of them lose far more later, on bets sized for the skill they believed they had rather than the skill they actually had, and neither one connected the size of that later loss to the story they'd been telling themselves since the win.

This isn't a book about people who are arrogant by nature. Most are careful, self-aware in every other part of their lives — parents who double-check the car seat, friends who'd never brag about anything else. Something specific happens the moment a bet pays off, something that doesn't require arrogance to begin with and produces something close to it by the end. I wanted to understand that one narrow, financial version of it.

I have a personal stake in getting this right, because I've been the person telling the flattering story. One decision landed well enough, early enough, that I built a small private mythology around my own judgment — a mythology that survived, undisturbed, for longer than it deserved to. Writing this wasn't an act of distance from that mistake. It was an act of finally looking at it straight on.

This book won't tell you to distrust every good decision you make. Some of them really were good decisions, made with real skill. What it will do is hand you a way to tell the difference — between the win that means something and the win that just means you got lucky and haven't been billed for it yet.

Introduction

Picture the exact moment it happens: not the win itself, but the half-second right after it, when a result that could have gone either way has just gone your way, and something in your head quietly starts writing the story of why. You didn't get lucky. You saw something. You read the signal, trusted your gut, held your nerve when someone more cautious would have folded — and it worked, and the working feels like proof. Nobody hands you that story. You write it yourself, in real time, usually before the money has even finished clearing, and you write it so convincingly that by the time the next opportunity arrives, you've forgotten it was ever a story at all. It's just what happened. You're good at this.

This book is about what happens next, because "you're good at this" is rarely where the story stops. It's where the story starts pricing your next decision, and your next one after that, each bet a little larger than the last, each larger bet justified by a track record that, examined honestly, is usually shorter and shakier than the confidence built on top of it. This isn't a book about fear, and it isn't a book about money that arrives and disappears too fast. It's about the opposite kind of danger — the one that shows up disguised as competence, that gets stronger with every win instead of weaker, and that feels, from the inside, exactly like getting smarter, right up until it doesn't.

Here is the thesis this whole book is built to defend, stated as plainly as it can be stated: **winning teaches your brain that you're the reason good things happen, and that lesson gets more dangerous every time chance confirms it for free.** Losing gets explained away — bad luck, bad timing, a market nobody could have predicted. Winning gets absorbed as evidence of skill, filed away as proof of an edge that, for most people in most situations, was never actually established by anything more rigorous than a favorable roll of the dice. You don't need to be reckless for this to happen to you. You don't need to be uninformed, or young, or new to whatever game you're playing. You only need to have won once, under conditions ambiguous enough that skill and luck were both plausible explanations — which describes the overwhelming majority of financial wins anyone ever experiences — and to have quietly picked the explanation that felt better.

Consider someone in the early months of a first serious attempt at picking individual stocks, working from a modest account built over several years of steady saving, who buys into a company after reading about it for a single weekend and watches the position climb faster and further than anything else in the portfolio over the following two months. There was no elaborate analysis behind the purchase — a headline, a hunch, a conversation with a coworker who'd mentioned the name once. The climb that followed had almost nothing to do with any of that; it was driven by a broader run in the sector that lifted dozens of comparable companies at once, a fact that would have been obvious from a slightly wider chart, a fact this person never checked, because checking it wasn't the instinct the win produced. The win produced a different instinct entirely: a settled, comfortable certainty that the weekend of reading had actually mattered, that the hunch had been a genuine read rather than a coin flip that happened to land right side up, and that the sensible next step was to do it again, with more money, and less reading.

Consider a second person, further along in a different kind of risk-taking: a small-business owner who makes an unusually aggressive expansion decision — a second location, financed heavily, opened faster than any advisor would have recommended — and watches it succeed beyond anything reasonable planning would have projected, carried substantially by a wave of local development that had nothing to do with the owner's own judgment and everything to do with timing nobody in the room could take credit for. The owner doesn't experience it that way. The owner experiences a specific, personal vindication: proof that betting bigger, faster, and with less hedging is simply how growth actually works for someone with real instincts for this business, a lesson that gets applied, two years later, to a third location opened under conditions the first two never had to survive — worse timing, thinner margins, a market that had already absorbed what growth it had to give — financed just as aggressively, on the strength of a confidence that was never actually earned by the first two decisions in the way it felt like it was.

These two people are doing the identical thing, in domains that look nothing alike on paper: converting a single favorable outcome, produced substantially by conditions outside their control, into a durable belief about their own personal skill — a belief that then gets used to justify a larger, riskier version of the same bet, made with less caution than the original, because the original's success has been reclassified, retroactively, as evidence rather than luck. Neither of them is unusual. This is closer to the default setting of the human mind operating under uncertainty than it is to a personal flaw unique to either of them, and understanding why requires understanding a specific, well-documented piece of psychology this book spends its chapters unpacking: the difference between an outcome and the evidence that outcome actually provides about the decision that produced it.

Precision matters here, early, about what this book is not — because two other, closely related ideas live right next door to this one, and confusing them would blur the exact distinction this book exists to sharpen. This is not a book about panic, or about the acute, fear-driven impulse to flee at the first sign of danger — that reflex runs in the opposite emotional direction entirely, triggered by threat rather than by triumph, and it belongs to its own separate study. This is also not a book about what happens to money that arrives without effort attached to it, the way a windfall gets treated as less real and spent faster simply because of how it showed up. This book's subject doesn't care how the money arrived. It cares about what happens to your sense of your own judgment after a bet you made, however it was funded, pays off — and how that inflated sense of judgment then goes looking for a bigger bet to prove itself on again.

The mechanism this book names has a specific, technical home in psychology: self-attribution bias, sometimes called the self-serving bias, the well-documented tendency to credit successes to your own stable, internal qualities — skill, insight, discipline — while attributing failures to external, unstable factors outside your control — bad luck, bad timing, someone else's mistake. This isn't a moral failing. It's closer to a structural feature of how human beings process feedback about their own competence, present in some measurable form in nearly everyone, activated most powerfully in exactly the domains where the actual ratio of skill to luck is hardest to see clearly — and few domains hide that ratio better than investing, trading, or any bet-sized decision made under real uncertainty, where the same decision can produce wildly different outcomes depending on factors nobody in the room controlled or could have predicted.

Here's what makes this particular pattern especially dangerous compared to some of its cousins: it doesn't feel like a bias while it's operating. It feels like learning. Every other pattern in this library involves some version of a person doing something they already suspect, on some level, isn't quite rational — flinching at a red number they know intellectually will likely recover, spending a windfall they know is exactly as real as a paycheck. This one doesn't come with that quiet internal friction. Believing you're good at something you're actually good at feels identical, from the inside, to believing you're good at something you're not. There's no warning sensation attached to the mistake, no discomfort to alert you that something's off, which is exactly why this instinct can run for years, compounding one confirming win at a time, before the bet finally sized wrong enough to reveal what was never actually there.

Consider a third scene, because it's worth seeing this pattern operate somewhere further from stocks and storefronts. A recreational poker player, a few years into playing regularly with the same small group of friends, goes on a genuine hot streak across several consecutive sessions — largely, as an honest count of the hands would reveal, because the cards themselves ran unusually favorably during that stretch, not because anything about the player's decision-making had meaningfully sharpened. The player doesn't experience the streak as luck running favorably. The player experiences it as arrival — the sense of having finally figured something out, crossed some threshold from amateur instinct to real skill, a threshold that, examined honestly against the actual hand histories, was never crossed at all. What follows is a familiar shape: larger buy-ins, looser calls justified by a read the player is now sure is reliable, a willingness to sit through losing stretches that would once have prompted a pause, because the player has recoded those losses as temporary noise around an underlying skill level that was, in reality, never as high as the hot streak made it feel.

This particular instinct deserves an entire book of its own rather than a chapter tucked inside some broader survey of financial overconfidence, and it helps to pause on why. Overconfidence, described in general terms, is a wide, almost unmanageable subject — it touches how people plan their time, how they estimate their own health risks, how they judge their own driving. This book is narrower than that, deliberately. It's about one specific circuit: a financial win, ambiguous enough that luck was plausibly involved, converted into a durable belief about personal skill, spent on a larger subsequent bet. That circuit shows up across an enormous range of financial contexts — a trading account, a small business, a real estate portfolio, a poker table, a corporate boardroom — but it's the same circuit every time, which is exactly what makes it worth isolating and studying on its own terms rather than folding it into a broader, vaguer conversation about confidence in general.

It's also worth naming a specific reason this pattern has received less popular attention than some of its cousins in this library. A book about panic-selling or reckless windfall spending describes behavior most readers can recognize immediately as a mistake, even in the moment it's happening — there's a felt sense, faint but present, that something is going wrong. This pattern doesn't offer that same internal alarm. A person riding an escalating string of wins, each one reinforcing the last, typically feels not worse but better with each passing decision — sharper, more capable, more in control — right up until the specific bet that finally breaks the pattern. This is part of why overconfidence following a win is, dollar for dollar, one of the more expensive patterns in this entire library: it doesn't get interrupted by discomfort the way fear-driven or grief-driven spending sometimes does, because there's no discomfort present to interrupt it. The only thing capable of interrupting it is a deliberate, structural habit built in advance — which is the entire project the following nine chapters are built to help you construct.

This is the shape every chapter in this book will return to, wearing a different specific costume each time: a favorable outcome, produced by some mixture of genuine skill and plain chance in a ratio that's almost never as clean as it feels, gets absorbed entirely as evidence of skill, and that inflated sense of skill gets spent on a bigger, riskier version of the same bet. Chapter 1 looks at the basic architecture of the pattern — the scoreboard your mind keeps that only really counts the wins as data about you. Chapter 2 looks at the specific, well-studied illusion that makes random outcomes feel controllable the moment you're personally involved in producing them. Chapter 3 looks at the belief in streaks — the conviction that a run of wins means something is currently working, when the run itself is frequently indistinguishable from ordinary statistical noise. Chapter 4 looks at the near-universal belief that you're better than most people at whatever you're doing, a belief the math says can't be true for everyone holding it, and yet very nearly everyone holds it anyway. Chapter 5 looks at how a near-loss, a bet that almost failed but didn't, gets processed by the brain as its own kind of validating win. Chapter 6 looks directly at the escalation itself — how a win produces not just a feeling, but a measurable, well-documented increase in trading frequency and bet size. Chapter 7 looks at the story-editing that happens after a loss, the quiet retroactive rewrite that keeps the loss from ever counting as real evidence against your skill. Chapter 8 looks at what happens to feedback-seeking itself once someone believes they've already arrived — the specific way expertise, real or imagined, can make a person stop checking their own work at exactly the moment checking matters most. And Chapter 9 closes the book by following the pattern all the way to its largest, most expensive stage: the founder, the executive, the serial risk-taker who bets the whole enterprise a second time on the strength of a first win that was never quite what it appeared to be.

Here's a simple, concrete way to picture what this book is actually claiming, because the abstract version — "skill and luck get confused" — can slide past a reader without really landing. Picture a hundred people, none of them with any real edge at all, each flipping a coin ten times and betting on the outcome each time. Pure chance alone guarantees that some meaningful number of those hundred people will land an unusually favorable run — six, seven, even eight wins out of ten — through nothing more than the ordinary variance any large group of coin-flippers produces. Every one of those lucky flippers has access to the identical, compelling internal experience the trader, the poker player, and the founder in this book's scenes all describe: a felt sense of having read something correctly, of having a genuine touch for it, built entirely from a run that a coin had no opinion about at all. This isn't a cynical claim that no financial decision ever involves real skill — plenty do. It's a much narrower, more useful claim: that a favorable run, on its own, without additional evidence, cannot tell you which kind of run you're actually in. The coin-flipper and the genuinely skilled trader can produce identical-looking winning streaks, and the streak itself carries no information capable of telling them apart. Something else has to do that work. This book is about what that something else actually is, and how to build it before the streak arrives.

Plainly, then: here is what this book is not trying to do, because the opposite failure mode — becoming paralyzed by self-doubt after every win, refusing to ever trust your own judgment again — is not the goal here and would be its own kind of overcorrection. Some people really do have a genuine, durable edge in some specific domain, built through years of deliberate practice and honest feedback, and this book has no interest in talking a genuinely skilled person out of trusting real skill. The entire task ahead is narrower and more useful than blanket self-doubt: learning to tell the difference between a result that actually reflects your judgment and a result that mostly reflects the conditions you happened to be operating in, so that the confidence you carry forward into your next decision is sized to the evidence that actually supports it, rather than to how good the last win happened to feel.

One thing worth knowing before the first chapter begins, because it will make everything that follows easier to use rather than merely interesting to read: every chapter in this book follows the same structure, on purpose. A close scene or two, drawn from an anonymous, composite version of the pattern rather than any single real person. A section naming the actual, credited research behind the mechanism — never an invented statistic, never a study that doesn't exist, because a book about overconfidence has no business padding its own credibility with the same kind of unearned certainty it's trying to warn you about. A section counting what the pattern actually costs, in dollars and in the quieter currency of judgment eroded over time. And a set of concrete overrides, ending in one sentence built to be remembered on the exact day you'll need it — not the calm day you're reading this, but the day some result, ambiguous and flattering, is trying to tell you a story about your own skill that the evidence doesn't yet support.

A word on how to read this book, since it's built to serve two somewhat different readers, and it's worth being honest about which one you might be. If you're reading this in the aftermath of a specific loss, trying to understand how you arrived at a bet that in hindsight looks obviously oversized, you may be tempted to read only the chapter that seems to describe your specific situation and set the rest aside. That's a reasonable instinct, and each chapter is genuinely built to stand on its own. But there's a real cost to reading only one chapter here, because the actual value of this book isn't any single mechanism — it's recognizing that all nine are the same underlying circuit, wearing different clothes, which means the specific trigger that gets you next time will very likely not be the one described in whichever chapter happened to match your last mistake. If you're reading this instead in a calmer moment, with no specific recent loss driving the search, you're in an even better position to get real use from these chapters, because the overrides in each one work considerably better built in advance than reconstructed after the fact, under the emotional pressure of a fresh, expensive lesson.

It helps to say plainly, too, who this book is not written for, because misapplied caution can cost a person just as much as misapplied confidence. If you're someone who has never taken a meaningful financial risk in your life, who declines every opportunity out of a generalized, undifferentiated fear rather than a specific, evidence-based caution, this book is not an argument for staying that way. Genuine opportunity requires genuine risk-taking, and a life spent entirely avoiding any bet at all is its own kind of costly mistake, just one this particular book isn't built to address. What follows is written specifically for the reader who takes risk, sometimes wins, and needs a way to tell the difference between the win that means something and the win that doesn't — not for the reader who's never given a bet a chance to prove anything either way.

Let's start where the whole pattern starts: not with the bet, and not with the outcome, but with the story your mind tells about the outcome the instant it's known — the scoreboard that keeps score of one thing only, and counts, without fail, every single win as yours.

Chapter 1 — The Scoreboard That Only Counts Wins

How Your Mind Keeps Two Different Sets of Books on Your Own Track Record

He remembers the trade that made him money in specific, vivid detail — the exact reasoning that led him to it, the chart pattern he noticed before anyone else on the forum he followed, the moment of conviction right before he clicked buy. He can tell the story unprompted, has told it more than once, and it always comes out sounding like a small case study in disciplined analysis: he saw something real, trusted it, and got rewarded for trusting it. He does not remember, with anything like the same clarity, the four trades before it that lost money on an almost identical setup, using an almost identical read of an almost identical chart pattern. When asked about those, months later, by a friend who happened to remember them because she'd watched him make each one, he pauses, genuinely searching, before landing on a flat, generic answer: the market was choppy that quarter. Nothing specific. Nothing that required a story, because those trades never got promoted to the category of things that explain who he is as an investor. They got filed, almost instantly and almost without his awareness of filing them, under noise — bad luck, bad timing, conditions outside anyone's control — while the one win got filed under signal: proof, finally, of a read he'd apparently had all along.

This is the mechanism the whole book is built around, and it's worth seeing it in its plainest form before any of the more specific costumes it wears in later chapters. Ask this same person to describe his own trading skill on a scale of one to ten, and he'll answer with a number built almost entirely from the win column of a ledger he never consciously chose to keep unevenly — a ledger where wins get a detailed autobiography and losses get a one-line dismissal, so that the final tally, whatever it actually says about his real track record, always seems to point toward a skill level higher than an honest, complete accounting would support.

A second scene shows the identical mechanism operating in a domain with no charts, no tickers, nothing that looks remotely like trading. A woman who runs a small consulting practice lands a large new client after what she describes, in the story she tells at every networking event since, as "trusting her instinct" during a pitch meeting where she deviated from her prepared materials on the spot. The client signed. The story of that pitch has become, in her own mind and in the mind of everyone who's heard her tell it, a small parable about the value of instinct over preparation — proof that she has a gift for reading a room that her more buttoned-up competitors lack. What the story omits, because she genuinely no longer thinks about it, is the previous year's pitch, delivered with an almost identical improvisational style to a different, larger prospect, which went nowhere — a loss she attributed, at the time and ever since, to the prospect "not being ready" for what she was offering, a factor entirely external to her own approach. Same instinct, deployed twice, one win and one loss, and only the win survived as a data point about who she actually is as a professional.

A third scene widens the picture to a domain many people wouldn't initially think of as involving financial risk at all, which is exactly why it's useful here. A man in his forties who's spent a decade managing his own retirement account rather than using a professional advisor keeps an informal mental tally of his decisions that he'd describe, if asked, as roughly even —

some good calls, some bad ones, a track record he considers solidly above average overall. Pressed to actually list five specific decisions from memory, he produces, without much effort, three genuine wins in vivid, confident detail, each one narrated as a case of good judgment rewarded. He struggles considerably longer to produce even two losses, and when he finally does, both come out heavily qualified — one blamed on a specific piece of bad news nobody could have anticipated, the other described as "not really a mistake, more like bad timing that would have worked out fine given another year." Neither loss gets described the way the wins were described: as evidence about his own decision-making. Both get externalized, softened, or reframed as something other than what they actually were, which is a loss produced by the same decision process that also, elsewhere, produced wins he's perfectly comfortable taking full personal credit for.

A fourth scene shows the same ledger operating across a much longer stretch of time, which is where its real cost tends to accumulate. A retired schoolteacher who spent almost thirty years contributing modestly and steadily to a workplace retirement plan, making almost no active decisions along the way, experiences a single, unusual moment of active choice late in her working life: she shifts a meaningful portion of her account into a more aggressive allocation shortly before an unusually strong multi-year run in the broader market, a decision she made mostly because a friend mentioned doing something similar, with very little independent analysis behind it. The years that follow are genuinely excellent ones for her account, and by the time she retires, she has folded that one decision into her larger personal narrative as proof that she has "decent instincts" about money despite never having considered herself a natural investor. She does not weigh, in that same narrative, the two smaller, more cautious decisions she made in earlier years that turned out modestly worse than simply staying put would have — both of which she remembers, when pressed, as "not really decisions, just going along with what seemed sensible at the time," a framing that quietly exempts them from ever counting as evidence about her judgment at all. Decades of steady, unremarkable contribution get compressed into a single flattering story about one lucky, well-timed swing, simply because that swing is the only part of her financial history that ever felt, subjectively, like something she actively chose.

What's actually happening

The specific mechanism operating in these scenes has a name in psychology, and it's one of the more thoroughly replicated findings in the entire field: self-serving attribution bias, first documented in a foundational way by psychologists Dale Miller and Michael Ross in the mid-1970s, whose review of the existing experimental literature established that people systematically credit their successes to internal, stable factors — ability, effort, skill. Their review's evidence for the flip side of that asymmetry — attributing failures to external, unstable factors like bad luck, difficult circumstances, or other people's errors — was real but genuinely thinner than the evidence for the success-crediting half, a distinction worth keeping honest rather than presenting both halves of the pattern as equally well-established. The bias isn't limited to any one domain; it's been documented across academic performance, athletic competition, workplace evaluation, and financial decision-making, and it shows up with remarkable consistency regardless of how intelligent, self-aware, or generally humble the person exhibiting it otherwise is. Miller and Ross's central contribution was showing that this asymmetry isn't simply people lying to themselves in some crude, conscious way — it reflects a genuine, largely unconscious asymmetry in how success and failure get processed and stored as information about the self, one that operates well below the level most people would notice happening in their own thinking.

It helps to understand why this asymmetry would exist at all, since it doesn't obviously serve accuracy — the one thing you'd think a decision-making system would be optimized to protect. The honest answer researchers have converged on involves motivation as much as cognition: maintaining a positive, coherent sense of your own competence appears to matter enormously for psychological functioning — for confidence, for persistence, for the willingness to keep trying difficult things after a setback — and a decision-making system that weighted every failure as equally informative as every success would likely produce a person too discouraged to keep functioning after a normal run of ordinary bad luck. Some asymmetry, in modest amounts, may genuinely serve a useful psychological purpose: it keeps people trying. The trouble, for the specific subject of this book, is that the amount of asymmetry this mechanism actually produces isn't modest. It's large enough to systematically distort a person's read of their own track record in exactly the domain — financial risk-taking — where an accurate read matters most, because the next decision's size gets calibrated directly against the story this asymmetric ledger is telling.

A related piece of the mechanism deserves a closer look, because it explains why the losses in all three scenes above got not just minimized but actively reclassified rather than simply forgotten. Psychologists studying causal attribution more broadly — building on earlier foundational work by Fritz Heider and later formalized by Bernard Weiner into a fuller theory of achievement-related attributions — distinguish between internal and external causes, and separately between stable and unstable ones. A win attributed to skill is internal and stable: it says something enduring about who you are, and it's expected to recur, because skill doesn't evaporate between one decision and the next. A loss attributed to bad luck is external and unstable: it says nothing about who you are, and there's no reason to expect it to recur, because luck, by definition, is not a persistent property of the person experiencing it. This four-way sorting isn't random — it's specifically the sorting that protects a stable, positive self-image most efficiently, which is exactly why it recurs so reliably across completely unrelated domains of a person's life, from pitch meetings to poker tables to retirement accounts.

Financial decision-making is unusually fertile ground for this particular bias to operate largely unchecked, compared to domains with faster, cleaner feedback — and it's useful to be specific about why. A tennis player who insists a loss was purely bad luck gets corrected quickly and repeatedly by an opponent who's visibly, demonstrably better — the feedback loop is tight, public, and hard to argue with. A financial decision rarely offers feedback that clean. The same trade can lose money for reasons that really were external — a broad market move, a piece of unrelated news, timing nobody could have called — which means the self-serving explanation isn't always wrong, and its occasional accuracy is precisely what makes it so easy to apply indiscriminately even when it's wrong. Ambiguity is the soil this bias grows best in, and few domains offer more genuine, honest ambiguity about what actually caused a given outcome than a financial market where thousands of factors move at once, any one of which can plausibly be blamed for a result that had far more to do with the decision itself than the person walking away from it wants to believe.

A further layer comes from research on hindsight bias conducted by psychologist Baruch Fischhoff, whose experiments demonstrated that once people know how something turned out, they consistently overestimate how predictable that outcome actually was beforehand — a phenomenon sometimes summarized as the "knew it all along" effect. Applied here, this compounds the self-serving asymmetry directly: not only does a win get filed as evidence of skill, but the reasoning that led to the win retroactively gets remembered as clearer and more confident than it actually was at the time the decision was made. The trader who "saw something real" in that chart pattern likely felt considerably less certain in the actual moment of clicking buy than his retold version of the story now suggests — hindsight has quietly sharpened a genuinely ambiguous, uncertain decision into a confident, foresighted one, after the fact, without his conscious awareness that any editing has occurred.

One more piece explains why this asymmetric ledger tends to get more entrenched over time rather than less: confirmation bias, one of the most extensively studied tendencies in cognitive psychology, describes the general human preference for information that supports an existing belief over information that challenges it. Once someone has settled into a self-image built substantially on a flattering, uneven ledger — "I have good instincts for this" — that belief starts actively shaping what gets noticed and remembered going forward, not just what happened in the past. Ambiguous future outcomes get interpreted in whatever way is most consistent with the existing self-image; a mediocre result gets quietly reframed as a near-win, a genuine mistake gets reframed as bad luck, each new data point sorted on arrival by a filter the earlier, uneven ledger has already built. The bias doesn't just distort the historical record once. It keeps distorting every new entry added to it, which is part of why the schoolteacher's single lucky swing could calcify into "decent instincts" over the better part of a decade without a single moment of active reconsideration.

What it costs you

The most direct cost is the one every later chapter in this book will return to from a different angle: a track record that feels, subjectively, much stronger than it actually is produces confidence that's miscalibrated against real evidence, and miscalibrated confidence eventually gets spent on a bet sized for a skill level that was never actually demonstrated. The man with the retirement account, confident in an above-average track record built substantially from an uneven ledger, is likely to take on more risk in his next decision than an honest, complete accounting of his actual history would support — not because he's reckless, but because the version of his history he's carrying around in his head genuinely isn't the same as the version a neutral third party, working from the full record, would produce.

There's a subtler cost that compounds over a much longer timeframe: the asymmetric ledger doesn't just distort confidence in the moment. It actively degrades the quality of feedback a person could otherwise be learning from. Genuine improvement in any skill-based domain depends on accurately identifying what specifically went wrong when something goes wrong, so the specific error can be corrected rather than repeated. A person who reflexively externalizes every loss — bad timing, bad luck, a market nobody could have predicted — never actually performs that diagnostic work, because the loss never gets treated as data worth diagnosing in the first place. This means the same underlying mistake, whatever it actually is, can recur indefinitely, protected from correction by a ledger that keeps recategorizing it as something other than a mistake every single time it happens.

A third cost shows up specifically in how this pattern affects other people's trust over time, particularly in shared financial decisions — a marriage, a business partnership, a family investment made together. A partner who consistently tells a version of shared financial history where their own calls get credited and their own misses get externalized, while the other partner's calls receive no similar generosity, produces a quiet, compounding erosion of trust that rarely gets named directly, because it doesn't look like dishonesty from the inside. It looks, to the person doing it, like an accurate accounting of what actually happened — which is precisely what makes it so difficult for a partner on the receiving end to challenge without the conversation curdling into something that feels, to the first person, like an unfair personal attack rather than a legitimate correction to a genuinely lopsided record.

A fourth, slower-moving cost deserves its own mention, because it explains why this pattern is so easy to miss in the moment and so obvious only in retrospect, often at exactly the moment it's least affordable to discover. A person operating from an inflated sense of their own track record tends to under-save relative to the risk they're actually taking on, reasoning, whether consciously or not, that their above-average judgment will make up the difference over time in a way a more cautious, honestly self-assessed person wouldn't assume. This isn't a single bad decision — it's a background assumption baked into years of smaller choices about how much of a cushion to keep, how aggressively to allocate, how much to lean on future skill rather than present caution. The cost of that assumption rarely shows up as a single dramatic event. It shows up, much later, as a gap between the financial security a person assumed their judgment had earned them and the financial security an honest, complete accounting of their actual decisions would have produced.

How this shows up without you noticing

The clearest tell is a specific asymmetry in how long a story takes to tell. Notice, the next time you or someone close to you describes a financial decision, how much detail accompanies a win versus a loss. A win tends to arrive with a beginning, middle, and end — the specific signal noticed, the reasoning followed, the moment of conviction, the payoff. A loss, when it gets mentioned at all, tends to arrive compressed into a single clause, often trailing off into something vague: "that one didn't work out," "the market turned," "bad timing." That compression isn't a neutral fact about which stories happen to be more interesting to tell. It's the ledger itself, operating in real time, visible in nothing more than which stories get the long version and which get the short one. A second, quieter tell shows up in how quickly a win gets folded into a general statement about identity — "I'm good at this," "I have an eye for it" — versus how rarely an equivalent loss ever gets folded into an equally general statement in the opposite direction. Nobody spontaneously concludes "I'm bad at this" from one loss the way they conclude "I'm good at this" from one win, and that asymmetry alone is worth listening for in your own internal narration.

The overrides

Keep a written record before the outcome is known, not after. The single most effective corrective to an asymmetric memory is removing memory from the equation entirely. Before any meaningfully sized financial decision, write down — in a notebook, a document, anywhere you'll actually look at it again — your specific reasoning and your honest confidence level at the time, before you know how it turns out. This isn't about predicting the future more accurately. It's about creating a record your later, outcome-biased memory can't quietly rewrite, so that six months from now you're comparing your actual reasoning against the actual result, rather than comparing a flattering reconstruction against a result you already know.

Review your losses with the same narrative effort you give your wins. Once a quarter, or after any significant loss, sit down and write the loss's story with the same level of specific, honest detail you'd naturally give a win — what you were thinking, what information you had, what you'd do differently. If you find yourself reaching for a one-line external explanation where a win would have gotten three paragraphs of internal credit, that gap is the bias itself, made visible enough to work against.

Ask what a neutral stranger, reading only the numbers, would conclude about your track record. Strip away your own narration entirely and imagine handing your actual decision log — not your memory of it, the written record — to someone with no stake in flattering you. What would they conclude about your actual skill level, based purely on the outcomes and the reasoning recorded at the time? That imagined outside read is usually a far more accurate gauge than anything your own memory will hand you unprompted.

Track your calibration, not just your outcomes. Alongside each recorded decision, note your stated confidence level at the time — not just what you decided, but how sure you said you were. Over enough decisions, compare your stated confidence against your actual results: if you consistently claimed high confidence on calls that turned out roughly fifty-fifty, that gap is worth taking seriously as information about how reliable your gut sense of your own certainty actually is.

If you share financial decisions with a partner, ask them to name the pattern, and actually listen. People closest to you often see the asymmetry in your own storytelling far more clearly than you do, precisely because they were present for both the wins you claim credit for and the losses you've quietly externalized. Ask directly, in a calm moment, whether they've noticed you telling your financial story unevenly — and treat the answer as useful data, not as an accusation to defend against.

Before treating any win as evidence of skill, ask what would have had to be true for it to fail instead. If the honest answer involves factors entirely outside your control — a sector-wide rally, a lucky break in timing, conditions that could easily have gone the other way — the win is weaker evidence about your own judgment than it feels like in the moment, regardless of how satisfying the story sounds when you tell it.

Give every loss the same amount of retelling time as your best win, out loud, at least once. Pick your single favorite success story — the one you tell most often — and, in the same sitting, tell the story of your worst loss with equal length and equal detail. Most people find this considerably harder to do than they expect, and the difficulty itself is useful information about how lopsided the underlying ledger actually is.

Set a recurring, dated review of your full decision log, not just the memorable entries. Once a quarter, read through your entire written record in order, start to finish, rather than skimming for the parts you remember fondly. A full, chronological read surfaces entries an uneven memory would otherwise have quietly dropped.

Watch for confirmation bias actively shaping how you interpret ambiguous new outcomes, not just how you remember old ones. Once you've built a self-image around a particular track record, notice whether an ambiguous new result gets automatically interpreted in whatever direction confirms that existing image. Deliberately consider the opposite interpretation before settling on the flattering one — a small habit that directly interrupts the mechanism by which an uneven ledger keeps reinforcing itself with every new entry.

Your memory is not a neutral witness to your own track record — it's a biased narrator with a clear preference for stories where you're the reason things go well. The only reliable defense is a written record made before the story gets a chance to write itself.

Chapter 2 — The Illusion of the Steering Wheel

Why Being Personally Involved in a Bet Makes It Feel Less Random Than It Actually Is

She picks her own numbers for the office lottery pool every single week, always the same six, chosen years ago for reasons she can no longer fully articulate — a birthday, a childhood address, a number that "felt right" the first time she wrote it down. When a coworker once suggested letting the machine generate a random set instead, saving everyone the trouble of remembering their picks, she resisted more strongly than the stakes could possibly justify, unable to name exactly why beyond a vague, stubborn sense that her own numbers gave her a better shot than a machine's numbers would. She knows, if asked directly and given time to think about it, that a random number generator produces exactly the same odds as any six numbers she could hand-pick. She does not feel that fact, in the moment of filling out the slip, with anything like the conviction she feels her own careful selection deserves.

This small, low-stakes habit is worth taking seriously, because it's a clean, uncontaminated example of a mechanism that shows up in a much more expensive form throughout the rest of this book: the sense that personal involvement in an outcome — choosing it yourself, rather than having it assigned to you — genuinely improves your odds, even in situations where the outcome is, by definition, entirely random and completely indifferent to who made the selection or how carefully they made it.

Consider a version of the same instinct with real money attached, and a great deal more of it. A man managing his own investment account insists on hand-selecting each individual position himself rather than using a diversified fund that would track the same broad market with far less effort and, by most honest measures, comparable or better long-run results. He describes his preference in terms of control — he wants to know exactly what he owns, wants the ability to act quickly if something changes, wants to feel like an active participant in his own financial outcomes rather than a passive rider on someone else's basket of holdings. What he's less able to articulate, because it operates well beneath the level of conscious reasoning, is a deeper and less defensible belief lurking underneath the stated preference for control: that his personal selection process, however informal, is actually improving his odds relative to a broad, low-cost alternative that requires no selection at all — a belief the actual data on individual stock-picking versus diversified index investing does not, in the aggregate, support nearly as strongly as his confidence in his own process would suggest.

A third scene shows the mechanism in a domain designed, almost deliberately, to exploit it. A man playing a slot machine at a casino consistently chooses to pull a physical lever rather than press the equivalent button, and consistently prefers machines that let him stop the spinning reels manually with a second button press rather than letting them resolve automatically — features the machine's designers know, from decades of behavioral research, increase a player's sense of personal involvement in the outcome without changing the actual, fixed odds by even a fraction of a percent. He plays longer, and bets more per spin, on machines offering this illusion of manual control than on otherwise identical machines that simply resolve automatically once a bet is placed — a difference in his own behavior he'd struggle to explain, since he'd readily agree, if you asked him directly and gave him a moment to think it through, that stopping the reels himself can't possibly change what symbols are already determined to land.

A fourth scene shows the illusion operating in a setting with no cards, no reels, and no tickers at all: a homeowner deciding whether to sell a property himself, without an agent, in a market he describes as "one I actually understand" because he's lived in the neighborhood for years and follows local listings closely as a hobby. He spends considerably more hours than a typical seller would on staging, pricing research, and negotiating directly with prospective buyers, driven by a conviction that his personal, hands-on involvement is meaningfully improving his outcome relative to simply hiring an experienced agent and stepping back. The home eventually sells for a price within the ordinary range comparable homes in the area fetched that season, agent or no agent — a result his hands-on effort, examined honestly, likely had very little to do with, since the local market's overall conditions were doing most of the actual work. He nonetheless describes the sale afterward as proof that his active, personal approach paid off, a conclusion the outcome alone can't actually support, since he has no comparison against what an agent-assisted, more hands-off sale of the identical property would have produced under the identical market conditions.

A fifth scene shows a milder, more everyday version of the same instinct, worth including because it demonstrates how ordinary and low-stakes this pattern can be while still shaping real financial behavior. A woman who insists on personally timing her monthly grocery shopping around specific sale cycles, tracking prices across three different stores rather than shopping at whichever is most convenient, describes the practice as meaningfully improving her household's finances — a genuine source of pride she brings up regularly in conversation. When she finally sits down, at a friend's suggestion, to actually calculate the total time invested against the actual dollar savings achieved, the hourly return on her effort turns out to be considerably below what she earns at her actual job, a comparison she'd never previously run because the active, hands-on feeling of getting a good deal had always felt, on its own, like sufficient evidence that the effort was paying off.

What's actually happening

This entire family of behavior has a specific, well-documented name in psychology: the illusion of control, first named and rigorously studied by psychologist Ellen Langer in a series of experiments beginning in the mid-1970s. Langer's research demonstrated, across a range of cleverly designed studies, that people consistently behave as though they have more influence over chance-determined outcomes than they actually do. For this book's purposes, the more important finding is that this illusion strengthens specifically when factors associated with genuine skill are artificially introduced into an otherwise purely random situation. In one of her most cited experiments, participants who were allowed to personally select their own lottery ticket, rather than having one handed to them at random, demanded significantly more money to sell that ticket back before the drawing than participants who'd simply been given a ticket — even though both tickets carried, by definition, identical odds. The act of choosing, all on its own, with nothing else different about the situation, measurably increased how much people valued a purely random outcome, as though the choosing itself had somehow improved their odds.

Langer identified several specific factors that reliably strengthen the illusion, and it's worth naming them directly because they show up, in various combinations, throughout the rest of this book's chapters: choice, where a person selects the outcome rather than having it assigned; familiarity, where the situation resembles one the person has genuine experience or skill in, even if that specific instance is actually random; competition, where the presence of a passive or less-engaged opponent makes the person's own active engagement feel more decisive than it actually is; and active involvement, where physically doing something — pulling a lever, clicking a button, timing an entry — makes the outcome feel produced by the person's own action rather than by chance operating independently of it. Financial markets, it's worth noting plainly, offer a nearly perfect combination of all four factors at once: you choose your positions, you're often at least somewhat familiar with the companies or sectors involved, you're implicitly competing against other market participants, and you actively click a button to execute every single trade. Few environments outside a casino floor are this well-suited to triggering the illusion of control at full strength, and unlike a casino floor, a brokerage account doesn't come with flashing lights reminding you that you're playing a game of chance.

There's a deeper mechanism worth understanding underneath Langer's original findings, developed in subsequent research: the illusion of control appears to be strongest precisely in situations that blend genuine skill elements with genuine chance elements in ambiguous proportions — situations, in other words, exactly like investing, where skill really can matter at the margins, but where the actual weight of skill relative to chance in any single outcome is nearly impossible to determine cleanly in real time. A purely random game, like a coin flip with no skill component whatsoever, produces a much weaker illusion of control than a game like stock-picking, where enough genuine expertise plausibly exists somewhere in the world — professional analysts, informed insiders, people who really do have an edge — that an amateur participant can reasonably believe their own effort is buying them a meaningful piece of that same edge, even when the actual evidence suggests their individual picks are landing closer to chance than to skill.

A related finding from research on financial decision-making specifically connects Langer's foundational work to the actual behavior of investors managing real accounts. Studies examining the relationship between an investor's sense of personal control and their subsequent trading frequency and risk-taking have found that investors who report feeling more personally in control of their outcomes — through active stock selection, frequent monitoring, or hands-on portfolio management — tend to trade considerably more often and take on measurably more concentrated risk than investors managing comparable sums through a more hands-off, diversified approach, without this increased activity translating, on average, into better returns. The felt sense of control appears to increase engagement and confidence substantially more than it increases actual outcomes, which is precisely the gap this chapter exists to name.

One final piece explains why the man at the slot machine and the man hand-picking his own stocks would both resist, if challenged, the idea that they're doing anything irrational. The illusion of control doesn't feel like an illusion from the inside — it feels like reasonable engagement with a situation you have some genuine stake in influencing. This is part of what makes it so durable: unlike a belief that's obviously false on its face, the illusion of control is usually wrapped around a kernel of genuine truth — you really can improve your odds through skill in some domains, and you really do have some legitimate influence in some financial decisions — which makes it extremely difficult to cleanly separate the situations where your involvement is actually buying you something from the situations where it's buying you nothing but a stronger, costlier conviction that it is.

A further, practically important wrinkle comes from research on what's sometimes called the "illusion of validity" — a related concept described by Daniel Kahneman in his broader writing on judgment under uncertainty. Kahneman observed that a person's subjective confidence in a judgment often depends far more on the internal coherence of the story they've built to support it than on the actual, statistical quality of the evidence behind it. A hand-picked stock, chosen after a coherent, satisfying process of reading, comparing, and deciding, produces a strong, confident feeling precisely because the process felt thorough and internally consistent — regardless of whether that process actually correlated with better outcomes than a much less thorough, essentially random alternative would have produced. The homeowner's hours of staging and research created exactly this kind of coherent, satisfying internal story, entirely independent of whether the story had any real bearing on the eventual sale price.

A further, useful nuance from Langer's own later work sharpens this point, since it sharpens rather than simply reinforces the earlier finding: subsequent research building on her original studies found that the illusion of control weakens measurably when a person is made explicitly aware, in advance, that an upcoming task is purely a matter of chance — the illusion, in other words, isn't perfectly immune to correction. It's simply that ordinary financial decisions almost never come pre-labeled as "chance" the way a laboratory coin flip does. A stock purchase looks, sounds, and feels like a skill-based decision, dressed in analyst reports and price charts and company names, which is precisely why the correcting effect Langer identified in her lab rarely gets a chance to operate in an actual brokerage account — nothing in the environment ever announces plainly that a given decision is, for this particular person in this particular instance, functionally closer to a coin flip than to a skill contest.

What it costs you

The most direct cost shows up in exactly the pattern the research on investor behavior describes: increased trading activity and increased concentration, both driven by a felt sense of personal control that isn't actually backed by a proportional increase in real predictive edge. Every additional trade carries real costs — transaction fees, tax consequences from short-term gains, the simple mathematical drag of trading more frequently than a strategy's actual edge, if any exists, can support — and an investor operating under a strong illusion of control tends to absorb all of these costs while believing, the entire time, that the increased activity is working in their favor rather than quietly eroding it.

There's a second cost that compounds specifically around the choice element Langer identified: a strong preference for hand-picking individual investments, driven partly by the illusion of control rather than purely by a rational assessment of expected returns, frequently comes at the expense of diversification — the well-established, unglamorous risk-management principle of spreading exposure across many holdings rather than concentrating it in a smaller number of positions a person feels personally confident about. Concentrated positions selected under an inflated sense of personal control carry more risk than a diversified alternative, and that additional risk rarely gets weighed honestly against the additional confidence the selection process produces, because the confidence itself is precisely what's clouding the risk assessment.

A third, quieter cost shows up in how this pattern affects a person's willingness to accept genuinely sound, less personally-controlled financial advice. Someone under the grip of a strong illusion of control often resists recommendations toward broader diversification or professional management specifically because those recommendations require surrendering the sense of active, personal involvement that feels, to them, like the actual source of their results — even when a more hands-off approach would, on the actual numbers, likely serve them better. The illusion doesn't just distort the decision itself. It distorts the person's willingness to even consider evidence that the decision might be worth reconsidering.

A fourth cost is the specific, easily overlooked one the home-sale scene illustrates: the illusion of control makes it nearly impossible to accurately evaluate your own past decisions, because you're never actually able to observe the alternative you didn't take. The homeowner has no genuine way of knowing whether his hands-on approach helped, hurt, or made no difference at all relative to hiring an agent, and in the absence of that comparison, the illusion fills the gap with the most flattering available conclusion by default. This isn't limited to real estate — it's a general feature of any actively-managed financial decision where the road not taken never gets to run, leaving the illusion of control free to claim credit for outcomes a more passive approach might well have matched or beaten.

How this shows up without you noticing

Listen for the specific language of preference dressed up as evidence: "I like to know what I own," "I want to be able to act fast," "I don't trust handing it off to someone else." None of these statements are unreasonable on their own terms, and none of them are, by themselves, evidence that active involvement is actually improving the outcome. The tell is whether the statement ever gets followed by an actual comparison — a real number, a real benchmark — or whether it simply stands alone as a closed, self-justifying preference nobody in the conversation, including the person speaking, ever thinks to test.

The overrides

Separate the decision to participate from the decision to control every input. Before making a financial decision that involves an unusually high degree of personal selection — an individual stock over a diversified fund, a specific timing decision over a scheduled one — ask directly whether the added control is actually buying you a demonstrated edge, or whether it's mostly buying you a stronger feeling of involvement. These are not the same purchase, and only one of them shows up in your actual returns.

Notice when familiarity is doing the work that skill should be doing. If your confidence in a particular pick or decision rests heavily on the fact that you recognize the company, the industry, or the situation, ask honestly whether that recognition translates into any actual predictive advantage, or whether it's simply making an otherwise uncertain bet feel more comfortable. Familiarity and edge are frequently confused for each other, and only one of them improves your odds.

Run a blind comparison against a random or automated alternative. Periodically compare the actual performance of your hand-selected decisions against what a simple, low-effort, largely random alternative — a broad index, a coin-flip allocation among a reasonable set of options — would have produced over the same period. If the hand-selected approach isn't reliably beating the low-effort alternative net of the extra time, cost, and risk it required, the illusion of control is likely costing you more than your own involvement is earning you.

Watch for the specific pull toward active involvement in moments of uncertainty. If you notice a strong urge to do something — check the account again, make a small adjustment, act in some way — specifically during a period of market uncertainty rather than in response to any new information, that urge is frequently the illusion of control seeking an outlet rather than a genuinely useful response to changed circumstances. Sitting still, in these specific moments, is often the harder and more correct choice.

Ask what a person with no ability to act would do differently. Imagine someone in your exact financial position who, for whatever reason, couldn't make any active trades or adjustments for the next year — only hold what they already have. Would that person's likely outcome actually be worse than yours, given your active involvement? If you're honest, the answer is frequently closer to even than your sense of your own contribution would suggest.

Notice when a decision has been explicitly labeled as chance, and let that label actually change your behavior. Some financial decisions genuinely are close to a coin flip — a highly speculative position, an outcome dependent on a single unpredictable event. When you can honestly identify one of these, treat the identification as real information, sized accordingly, rather than letting the ordinary feeling of active involvement quietly override the label you yourself just applied.

Separate the enjoyment of active involvement from its financial justification, and let both exist honestly. If you genuinely enjoy the process of researching and selecting your own investments — as a hobby, a form of engagement, a source of real satisfaction — that's a legitimate reason to keep doing it, as long as it's named as what it actually is rather than smuggled in as a claim about superior returns it may not be delivering.

Calculate an honest hourly rate for any actively-managed effort before crediting it with meaningful savings or gains. If a hands-on approach — comparison shopping, active trading, self-managed real estate — is genuinely producing a measurable financial benefit, divide that benefit by the actual hours invested and compare the result honestly against what your time is worth elsewhere. A number this concrete is far harder to wave away with a vague, comfortable sense that the effort is "obviously" worth it.

The steering wheel in your hands doesn't mean the road is going where you're steering it — in a genuinely random or largely random situation, holding the wheel changes how the ride feels, not where it ends up.

Chapter 3 — The Hot Hand That Isn't There

Why a Run of Wins Feels Like Momentum Even When the Math Says It's Noise

Four trades in a row have gone his way, each one closing green, each one a little larger than the last because each win has funded a bigger position on the next attempt. He describes this stretch, to anyone who'll listen, using language borrowed directly from sports — he's "on a run," he's "seeing it clearly right now," he's "in a groove" he intends to ride for as long as it lasts. The fifth trade, sized considerably larger than any of the first four, uses the exact same strategy that produced the previous four wins, deployed with less caution than trade one received, because trade five isn't really being evaluated on its own merits anymore. It's being evaluated as the next installment in a streak that has, in his mind, already established its own momentum — a momentum he genuinely believes is a real, currently active property of his own decision-making, rather than what an honest statistical review of four consecutive coin-flip-adjacent outcomes would actually suggest, which is nothing more than an ordinary, unremarkable run of the kind random processes produce constantly, with no bearing whatsoever on what comes next.

This is the specific pattern the chapter is built around, and it deserves its own close examination separate from the broader self-attribution mechanism in Chapter 1, because a hot streak does something the earlier chapters don't fully capture: it doesn't just make you feel good about a single past win. It makes you feel like something is *currently, actively working* — a state, a groove, a temporary elevation in your own skill that's happening right now and will keep paying off if you keep riding it, right up until the moment it stops paying off, usually well after the bet size has already grown considerably larger than the actual evidence for a genuine hot streak ever justified.

Consider a version of the same instinct playing out in a domain with no trades at all: a recreational sports bettor who correctly picks the outcome of five consecutive games using a mix of research and instinct, and who describes the run, afterward, not as an unusually favorable stretch of luck but as evidence that he's "figured something out" about how to read a particular league's matchups — a specific, durable skill he now believes he possesses and didn't possess a month earlier. His sixth bet, placed with meaningfully more money than any of the first five, loses. His seventh, placed with even more money on the theory that the loss was simply "a blip" in an otherwise intact hot streak, loses as well. By the time he stops to actually total his results across the full run, the five early wins — which felt, at the time, like the entire story — account for a smaller share of his total activity than the two subsequent losses that followed them, made larger specifically because the hot streak convinced him the sixth and seventh bets were safer than the first five had been, when in fact nothing about the underlying odds had changed at all between bet one and bet seven.

A different, quieter version shows up in a workplace setting rather than a betting one: a small-business owner who lands three unusually large clients in quick succession, each one arriving through a slightly different channel — one referral, one cold outreach that worked better than expected, one a stroke of pure timing — describes the stretch, in conversation with her business partner, as proof that the business has "hit its stride," language that implies something durable and ongoing rather than three independent, only loosely related pieces of good fortune. On the strength of that read, she approves a significant increase in overhead — new hires, a larger office lease, expanded marketing spend — sized to the assumption that the recent pace of client acquisition represents the business's new normal rather than an unusually favorable, likely temporary cluster. When the pace inevitably reverts toward its more ordinary long-run average over the following two quarters, the increased overhead doesn't revert with it, because overhead, unlike a betting position, can't simply be unwound the moment the streak that justified it cools off.

A fourth scene shows the same conviction taking hold somewhere considerably slower-moving than a poker table or a betting slip: a real estate investor who, over an eighteen-month stretch, buys and successfully flips three small rental properties in quick succession, each one purchased in a rising local market that was, by any honest accounting, lifting nearly every comparable property in the area regardless of who owned it or how it was renovated. He describes the run, in conversation with a nephew considering following the same path, as evidence that he's "developed an eye" for undervalued properties in this specific market — a specific, personal skill he believes he's sharpened across the three deals, distinct from the broader market conditions that, on a fair reading of the timeline, accounted for the overwhelming majority of each property's appreciation. His fourth purchase, made with a considerably larger loan and a shorter planned holding period than any of the first three, closes just as the same local market begins to cool — a turn that was already visible in slowing sale times and softening asking prices before his fourth purchase closed, information he had access to and largely discounted, because the streak itself had become, by that point, more persuasive to him than the data describing the market it was actually happening inside of.

What's actually happening

The specific bias operating in these scenes is one of the most famous, and famously contested, findings in the entire field of behavioral decision science: the hot-hand fallacy, first rigorously studied by psychologists Thomas Gilovich, Robert Vallone, and Amos Tversky in a landmark 1985 paper that examined professional basketball shooting data alongside controlled experiments on both players and fans. Gilovich, Vallone, and Tversky found that basketball players and fans alike strongly believed a shooter who had just made several consecutive shots was more likely to make the next one than a shooter who had just missed several in a row — a belief so widely and confidently held across the sport that it shaped in-game strategy, commentary, and betting behavior. When the researchers actually analyzed real shooting records, they found no meaningful evidence supporting the belief: a player's chance of making a given shot was, in their original analysis, statistically indistinguishable whether the previous shots had gone in or missed. The "hot hand," at least by the measure their original study used, appeared to be a story people told about a sequence of outcomes that had no more actual momentum in it than a fair coin flipped repeatedly, which occasionally, purely by chance, produces streaks that look meaningful to a mind built to search for patterns.

This finding deserves an honest, complete accounting rather than the flattened version that circulated for decades, because the story of the hot-hand fallacy itself became a small case study in exactly the kind of overconfidence this book is about — researchers and popular writers alike treated the original 1985 finding as more settled than it actually was. A later, influential reanalysis by economists Joshua Miller and Adam Sanjurjo, published decades after the original study, identified a subtle statistical bias in how the original hot-hand research measured streaks, and found that when this bias is corrected for, small but genuine hot-hand effects do appear to exist in some shooting data — considerably smaller than the popular belief in "hot hands" would suggest, but not strictly zero, either. The honest, current state of the research is more nuanced than either "hot hands are completely imaginary" or "hot hands are exactly as real as fans believe": there may be a small, real effect in some skill-based, low-randomness domains like basketball shooting, but it is vastly smaller than the confident, momentum-driven belief people actually hold. And for this book's subject, the point that matters most is this: the broader hot-hand literature consistently finds little to no comparable effect in domains dominated far more heavily by chance than a basketball shot — short-term stock price movements, sports betting outcomes, the turn of a card — though that specific comparison is this book's extrapolation from the general pattern in the research, not a direct finding of the Miller-Sanjurjo reanalysis itself. This book's central point survives that more careful reading intact: whatever small, genuine momentum might occasionally exist in the most skill-saturated of these domains, the confidence people place in a "hot streak" is reliably, measurably larger than any evidence — even the corrected evidence — can support, and the gap between that inflated confidence and the actual, modest reality is exactly where the costly bet sizing in every scene above comes from.

A deeper cognitive mechanism sits underneath the specific hot-hand finding, one that explains why the belief is so persistent even in domains, like coin flips or short-term price movements, where genuinely no serial dependence exists at all. Human pattern-recognition, honed across an evolutionary history where detecting real patterns in the environment — a predator's movement, a seasonal food source, a social alliance — carried enormous survival value, appears to be strongly biased toward finding patterns even in sequences generated by pure chance, a tendency researchers sometimes describe under the broader heading of apophenia, or more specifically here, the "law of small numbers" described by Daniel Kahneman and Amos Tversky in earlier work: the tendency to expect that small samples of random data will resemble the properties of the larger population they're drawn from far more closely than they actually do. A genuinely random process, over a short run, produces streaks — clusters of wins, clusters of losses — far more often than most people's intuitive sense of "randomness" expects, which means a real, ordinary run of four or five favorable outcomes in a row is exactly the kind of thing pure chance produces routinely, without needing any underlying momentum to explain it at all.

A related, practically important finding, specific to financial markets rather than basketball or coin flips, belongs here too: extensive research into short-term stock price momentum has found that, unlike a shooter's next attempt, some real, modest momentum does appear to exist in certain market contexts over certain timeframes — a genuinely more complicated empirical picture than either "markets are pure chance" or "past performance reliably predicts future performance" would suggest. This complexity is worth naming honestly rather than flattened into a simple takeaway, precisely because it's exactly the kind of ambiguous, partially-true middle ground the illusion of a personal hot streak thrives in. The existence of some genuine, modest, well-studied momentum effects in certain market conditions is not the same thing as evidence that any individual trader's personal four-trade winning stretch reflects a durable elevation in that specific trader's own skill — the two claims sound similar and are not remotely the same, and conflating them is precisely how a real, narrow, thoroughly-studied market phenomenon gets misapplied to justify an unjustified personal bet.

A further piece, connected to research on how streaks specifically interact with self-attribution, ties this chapter directly back to Chapter 1's mechanism. A run of favorable outcomes doesn't just feel like momentum in the moment — it actively strengthens the internal, stable attribution a person makes about their own skill, considerably more than a single isolated win would, because a streak reads as a pattern rather than an event, and patterns are exactly the kind of evidence a mind looking to confirm a stable personal trait is primed to seize on. The real estate investor's "eye" for undervalued properties felt more solidly established after three consecutive successful flips than it would have after just one, even though, statistically, three data points drawn from the same generally rising market provide barely more independent evidence of personal skill than one does — they're not really three separate tests of his judgment. They're one test, repeated three times under nearly identical favorable conditions, dressed up as three separate confirmations.

What it costs you

The most direct and measurable cost is the specific pattern visible in the sports bettor's story: bet or position sizing that grows across a streak, funded by the mistaken belief that the streak itself is informative about what comes next, means the largest bets of any given run are placed at exactly the moment the evidence for continued success is weakest — right after several wins, when reversion to an ordinary baseline is, if anything, the more statistically likely near-term outcome rather than continuation. This produces a specific, costly asymmetry: the wins that build the streak tend to be modestly sized, made with appropriate caution before any streak-based confidence has built up, while the losses that eventually end the streak tend to be comparatively large, made at exactly the moment overconfidence in the streak's durability had grown large enough to justify a larger bet.

There's a second cost visible in the business owner's story, one that's slower-moving and harder to reverse than a single bad trade: structural decisions — hiring, leases, expanded overhead — made on the assumption that a recent favorable run represents a new, durable baseline rather than a temporary cluster, saddle a business or a household with fixed costs sized for conditions that may not persist. Unlike a trading position, which can be closed the instant the streak cools, a lease or a salary commitment locks in an assumption about the future that becomes considerably more expensive to unwind once the underlying pace of results reverts to something closer to its ordinary average.

A third cost is psychological rather than financial, and it compounds specifically because a hot streak, statistically, is always eventually followed by a return toward the average — not because the streak "runs out," but because that's simply what an ordinary distribution of outcomes looks like over a longer run. A person who's built real personal identity around being "in a groove" experiences the inevitable reversion not as an unremarkable statistical event but as a personal failure, a loss of a gift they briefly had, which frequently triggers exactly the pattern Chapter 1 described — an urgent search for an external explanation that lets the earlier, flattering self-story stay intact, rather than an honest reassessment of how much the earlier streak actually reflected skill in the first place.

A fourth cost, specific to slower-moving domains like real estate or business expansion, is timing risk taken on precisely when the underlying conditions that produced the earlier streak are already turning, as they eventually always do. Because a streak-driven decision tends to be made with maximum confidence and minimum scrutiny at the exact point the streak has run longest, it also tends to be made closest to whatever eventual reversion is coming — which is precisely backwards from how caution should actually be allocated across a sequence of decisions made in a market or environment that, by its nature, cycles rather than climbs forever.

How this shows up without you noticing

The clearest tell is sports and momentum vocabulary showing up in a financial conversation: "on a run," "in a groove," "hot right now," "riding the wave." This language isn't decoration — it's doing real cognitive work, importing a felt sense of continuity and momentum into a domain where, for the overwhelming majority of everyday financial bets, no such continuity actually exists. Notice how naturally this vocabulary arrives after several wins in a row, and notice, too, how rarely an equivalent vocabulary of momentum gets applied after several losses in a row — nobody describes themselves as "in a cold streak that's clearly going to continue" with anything like the same confidence they bring to describing a hot one.

The overrides

Before increasing the size of any bet following a win, name the streak explicitly and ask what actually caused it. Write down, specifically, what you believe produced the recent run of favorable outcomes. If the honest answer is closer to "I don't actually know, but it's felt good" than to a specific, identifiable change in your process or information, treat the streak as statistically ordinary rather than as evidence of a currently elevated skill level.

Hold position or bet sizing constant across a streak unless you have a specific, articulable reason to change it. The single most direct defense against this pattern is refusing to let recent outcomes alone drive sizing decisions. If your process hasn't genuinely changed, your bet size shouldn't either, regardless of how many consecutive wins have just occurred — and if you find yourself wanting to increase size purely because of the streak itself, that impulse is precisely the bias this chapter describes, caught in the act.

Separate structural, harder-to-reverse decisions from position-level ones, and apply extra scrutiny to the structural ones. A trading position can be closed quickly if a streak reverts. A lease, a hire, or a expanded overhead commitment cannot. Apply a longer, more skeptical evaluation period before any structural decision gets justified by a recent favorable run, specifically because the cost of being wrong is so much harder to unwind than the cost of a single bad trade.

Look at the actual sequence, not just the summary. If you believe you're on a hot streak, write out the specific individual outcomes rather than relying on the general felt sense of "things going well lately." A written sequence is often far less impressive, and far more obviously ordinary, than the vague, flattering summary a person's memory tends to produce on its own.

Ask what would have to be true for this to be a real, durable skill improvement rather than an ordinary run. If you genuinely believe a recent streak reflects improved skill rather than luck, be specific about what changed in your process, your information, or your preparation that would explain the improvement. If nothing specific changed, the streak is almost certainly closer to noise than to a signal, however it feels in the moment.

Check whether the broader environment, not just your own decisions, moved favorably during the streak. Before crediting a run of wins to your own skill, look specifically at whether the wider market, sector, or local conditions were also moving favorably during the same window, for reasons unrelated to any individual choice you made. A rising tide lifting nearly everyone is a very different explanation than a personal edge, and the two are easy to confuse from inside a streak.

Pre-commit to a specific number of confirming instances before treating any pattern as real. Decide in advance how many independent, favorable outcomes you'd need to see before calling something a genuine skill improvement rather than an ordinary run — and hold yourself to that number, resisting the pull to declare victory early simply because the streak currently in progress happens to feel convincing.

Notice when a streak's momentum language starts shaping decisions outside the streak itself. If a run of wins in one area — a portfolio, a business line, a specific strategy — starts influencing your confidence or risk-taking in an unrelated area, treat that spillover as a warning sign rather than as evidence of a generally sharpened instinct. A genuine skill improvement in one narrow domain has no logical reason to increase your confidence anywhere else.

A hot hand feels like momentum from the inside, whether or not any real momentum exists — the only reliable way to tell the difference is to check the actual math instead of the feeling, every single time, especially the times the feeling seems most obviously right.

Chapter 4 — Everyone Thinks They're in the Top Half

Why Nearly Every Investor Believes Their Own Judgment Is Better Than Average

Ask a room full of investors, informally, to rate their own investing skill relative to other people in the room, and you'll get an answer that's mathematically impossible for the room as a whole to be right about: a strong majority will place themselves above the median, some considerably above it, and only a small handful will rate themselves as below average — even though, by the basic arithmetic of what "average" means, roughly half of any group necessarily falls below it. This isn't a quirk unique to investors. It shows up in study after study across an enormous range of skills and domains, and it's worth sitting with directly, because the specific version of it that shows up in financial risk-taking has an unusually direct, unusually expensive relationship to the size of the bets people are willing to make.

A man managing his own retirement account describes his investing approach, without prompting, as "better than what most people are doing" — not arrogantly, exactly, more as a simple, settled fact he's stopped examining, the same tone he'd use to describe his own eye color. Asked what he's actually comparing himself against, he can't point to any specific benchmark, any actual comparison of his returns against a broad market index or against other self-directed investors' documented results. The comparison isn't built from evidence. It's built from a general, diffuse sense that he pays more attention, thinks more carefully, and checks his positions more often than he imagines a typical person does — a set of behaviors he's equating, without ever quite examining the equation, with actually being better at producing results, when the underlying research on individual investor behavior suggests the opposite relationship holds at least as often: more frequent checking and more active trading tend to correlate with worse net results, not better ones, once costs are accounted for.

A second scene shows the same instinct playing out with real financial consequences attached to the comparison itself. A woman deciding whether to continue managing her own portfolio or move it to a professionally managed, diversified alternative reasons her way to keeping full control, in part, on the basis that she's "sharper than the average person these funds are designed for" — a comparison that implicitly assumes professionally managed funds are built as a floor for below-average investors rather than, as the actual evidence on long-run fund performance suggests, a genuinely competitive option that outperforms the majority of self-directed individual investors, including many who consider themselves considerably above average. She isn't comparing herself against the fund's actual documented performance. She's comparing herself against a vague, generic image of an unsophisticated investor that she's confident she doesn't resemble — a comparison built entirely from her own self-image rather than from any actual data about how her results have compared to the alternative she's declining.

A third scene shows the same comparison operating among people who, unlike the two above, actually do have access to real, direct evidence about how their results compare to others — and still manage to interpret that evidence in a self-flattering direction. A group of amateur investors in a monthly investment club regularly compares notes on returns, and one member, whose actual documented annual returns have landed in the middle of the group for three consecutive years running, nonetheless describes himself, in casual conversation outside the meetings, as "one of the sharper stock-pickers" in the club — a claim that isn't built from denying the actual numbers, which he could recite accurately if asked directly, but from a selective emphasis on the specific picks within his portfolio that performed best, treated as more representative of his overall skill than the picks that dragged his average down to the middle of the pack. He isn't lying about his results. He's simply weighting the evidence unevenly, the same way the ledger in Chapter 1 gets kept unevenly, until a middling documented record and a self-image as an above-average picker manage to coexist without much friction.

A fourth scene shows the belief operating on an entire profession rather than a single individual. A survey conducted informally among financial advisors at a regional conference, asking each attendee to rate their own client outcomes relative to their peers in the room, produces a strikingly familiar distribution: a large majority rate themselves in the top half, despite every advisor in the room being, definitionally, a peer of every other advisor in the room. When one presenter gently points this out from the stage, the room's response isn't embarrassment or reconsideration — it's a round of good-natured laughter, followed almost immediately by a return to the same settled confidence each advisor privately holds about their own specific practice, as though the math applied to the room in general but somehow not to any specific person currently sitting in it.

What's actually happening

The specific bias operating in these scenes is a well-documented finding sometimes called the better-than-average effect or illusory superiority, most famously demonstrated by the psychologist Ola Svenson in a 1981 study asking drivers to rate their own driving skill and safety relative to other drivers. Svenson found that a substantial majority of respondents rated themselves as above the median on both skill and safety — a result that is, by simple mathematical necessity, impossible for the group as a whole to be correct about, since a median by definition splits any distribution exactly in half. The finding has since been replicated across an enormous range of unrelated skills and traits — people rate themselves as above average at everything from job performance to ethical behavior to sense of humor — and it appears to be one of the more consistently reproducible findings in the entire field of self-assessment research.

Precision about what specifically causes this pattern matters, because the underlying mechanism has direct implications for financial decision-making that go beyond simple vanity. Subsequent research on self-assessment, notably a systematic framework developed by researchers Don Moore and Paul Healy, distinguishes between several genuinely distinct forms of overconfidence that had previously been lumped together under one general label. Overestimation is thinking you're better, in absolute terms, than you actually are. Overplacement is believing you rank higher relative to others than you actually do — the specific pattern Svenson's driving study measured. Overprecision is being more certain than the evidence warrants about the accuracy of your own beliefs and estimates. Moore and Healy's research found something particularly relevant to this book's subject: these three forms of overconfidence don't always move together, and in fact sometimes move in opposite directions depending on how difficult the task in question is perceived to be. On genuinely difficult, ambiguous tasks — a category that includes almost every meaningful financial decision made under real uncertainty — overplacement (believing you're better than most others) tends to be strongest precisely because the difficulty of the task makes accurate self-assessment hardest, and the resulting uncertainty gets filled in, by default, with a self-flattering estimate rather than a neutral or humble one.

A related mechanism, sometimes described as the "unique invulnerability" pattern in research on risk perception: people consistently rate their own personal risk of a wide range of negative outcomes — from health problems to relationship failures to financial losses — as lower than the average person's risk of the same outcome, even when given identical information about the actual base rates involved. Applied to investing specifically, this means an investor can genuinely understand, at an abstract level, that most individual investors underperform a simple diversified index over the long run — a well-documented, widely publicized finding — while simultaneously and comfortably believing that this well-known statistic simply doesn't apply to their own specific case, because they're not "most individual investors." The abstract statistic and the personal exemption from it coexist without much friction, because the exemption isn't reasoned through explicitly — it's assumed, quietly, as a background feature of how the person thinks about their own place relative to a generic, faceless average.

A further layer from research specifically on financial overconfidence and trading behavior connects this chapter directly to the broader escalation pattern this book is tracking. Studies examining the relationship between an investor's self-rated skill and their actual trading behavior have found that investors who rate themselves as more skilled than average — independent of whether their actual documented performance supports that self-rating — trade measurably more frequently and hold more concentrated positions than investors with more modest self-assessments. The overplacement isn't just a private, harmless belief sitting quietly in the background. It actively drives behavior, specifically toward more frequent, larger, and less diversified bets, precisely because a person who believes their own judgment outperforms the average investor's has a ready-made justification for deviating further from the cautious, diversified approach a more humble self-assessment would recommend.

A specific, sobering finding from research on gender differences in investor overconfidence and trading behavior, conducted by economists Brad Barber and Terrance Odean, belongs here, because it illustrates the practical stakes of overplacement with unusual clarity. Barber and Odean's research, examining large datasets of actual brokerage account activity, found that male investors, on average, traded considerably more frequently than female investors managing comparable accounts, and that this increased trading activity was associated with measurably lower net returns after accounting for transaction costs — a pattern the researchers connected directly to documented differences in average overconfidence levels between the two groups in their sample. The finding isn't a claim about any individual person's skill or judgment; it's a population-level illustration of exactly this chapter's mechanism in action: a group with, on average, higher self-rated confidence in their own financial judgment traded more, and that increased trading activity measurably cost them money rather than earning it, net of the costs the additional activity generated.

A related and important qualification matters here, since the honest reading of this research is more precise than a blanket claim that all confidence is misplaced. Later work examining the original gender-difference findings, along with broader research on overconfidence across different investor populations, has found that the size and even the direction of these effects vary depending on factors including investing experience, the specific market conditions studied, and how overconfidence itself was measured — and some researchers have raised legitimate questions about how consistently the original gap replicates across different samples and time periods. This book presents the finding as a genuine, well-documented illustration of overplacement's real behavioral consequences, not as a settled, universal law describing any particular group of investors — the core mechanism the research illustrates, that overplacement drives increased trading and increased trading tends to cost money, is the durable, well-supported part of the finding, independent of exactly how the effect distributes across any specific population.

A further, related piece connects overplacement directly to overprecision, the third form of overconfidence in Moore and Healy's framework. Overprecision — excessive certainty about how accurate your own estimates are — tends to compound overplacement's effects specifically in financial forecasting: an investor who not only believes they're better than average but also believes their own specific price targets and timing estimates are considerably more reliable than they actually are will size positions more aggressively around those estimates, taking on concentrated risk that a more honestly humble estimate of one's own precision would never justify. The two forms of overconfidence reinforce each other directly — believing you're above average makes your own estimates feel more trustworthy, and trusting your own estimates more makes the belief that you're above average feel more justified, a closed loop with very little room for outside correction to enter.

What it costs you

The most direct cost is the one Barber and Odean's research quantifies clearly: overplacement drives increased trading frequency, and increased trading frequency, net of transaction costs and tax consequences, tends to reduce returns rather than improve them for the overwhelming majority of individual investors, regardless of how confident any specific investor feels about their own above-average judgment in the moment. The cost isn't hypothetical or abstract — it's a measurable, well-documented gap between the returns an investor could have earned with a simpler, less active approach and the returns their actual, overplacement-driven activity produced.

There's a second cost specific to the decision, illustrated in the second scene above, to decline professionally managed or diversified alternatives on the basis of a felt sense of personal superiority rather than an honest comparison of actual documented results. An investor who assumes they're comparing favorably against a generic, unsophisticated benchmark, without ever actually running the comparison against real data, forgoes an alternative that, for a large majority of individual investors, genuinely does outperform self-directed active management over meaningful time horizons — a cost that compounds silently, year after year, precisely because it never gets measured against the road not taken.

A third cost is less financial and more social: illusory superiority, left unexamined, tends to make a person considerably less receptive to advice, correction, or genuinely useful feedback from people whose judgment might, in reality, be at least as sound as their own. If your baseline assumption is that your financial judgment already ranks above most people's, disagreement from a financial professional, a more experienced friend, or a partner starts to register less as useful information and more as a claim to be defended against — a posture that closes off exactly the kind of outside correction that could otherwise catch a mistake before it compounds into something expensive.

A fourth cost shows up specifically in how selective evidence-weighting, illustrated by the investment club member's story, distorts a person's ability to learn from a genuinely mixed track record. A middling record, honestly examined, contains real, useful information — which specific picks worked, which didn't, and why — that could meaningfully improve future decisions if actually studied. A middling record reinterpreted as an above-average one, by selectively emphasizing the strongest picks, forfeits that learning entirely, because there's no longer any perceived problem to investigate. The self-flattering read doesn't just misstate the past. It removes the incentive to ever look at the past closely enough to improve.

How this shows up without you noticing

Listen for comparisons that never name an actual reference group. "Better than most people" is a claim that sounds specific but rarely gets tested against an actual defined population — most people doing what, measured how, over what period. The clearest sign this chapter's bias is operating is a confident comparative claim that, when gently pressed for the specific benchmark it's being measured against, turns out to rest on nothing more concrete than a general, comfortable sense of being more careful or more attentive than an unspecified, imagined typical person.

The overrides

Ask for the actual comparison, not the felt one. Before concluding that your investing approach, or any specific financial decision-making process, is better than average, seek out the actual documented comparison — your own returns against a relevant benchmark, over a meaningful time period, net of costs — rather than relying on a diffuse, unmeasured sense of being more careful or more attentive than an imagined typical investor.

Notice when "better than average" is doing work that "correct" should be doing. A comparison against other people's presumed skill level is a different question entirely from whether your specific decision is a good one on its own terms. Even if you genuinely are a more skilled investor than most, that doesn't automatically mean your next specific bet is well-sized or well-reasoned — the two questions get conflated constantly, and only one of them actually protects you from a bad decision.

Run the numbers against a genuinely low-effort alternative, honestly, at least once a year. Compare your actual net returns, after all costs, against what a simple, broadly diversified, low-maintenance alternative would have produced over the same period. If you're not reliably beating that alternative, the belief that your active approach reflects above-average skill isn't supported by the one comparison that actually matters.

Treat a strong reaction to disagreement as a signal worth examining, not just enduring. If receiving pushback on a financial decision from a partner, friend, or professional produces a strong defensive reaction rather than genuine curiosity about whether they might be right, that defensiveness is worth noticing on its own terms — it's often a sign that illusory superiority has quietly become part of your identity rather than a casual, revisable opinion about your own skill.

Separate confidence in your process from confidence in your results. You can have real, well-earned confidence in a disciplined, thoughtful process — showing up, doing the research, thinking things through carefully — without that confidence extending automatically to a claim about how your actual results compare to other people's. Process discipline and above-average outcomes are related, but they are not the same claim, and conflating them is exactly how overplacement smuggles itself into an otherwise reasonable sense of self-respect about your own effort.

Ask what specifically you'd need to see to change your self-rating. If you believe you're an above-average investor, name in advance the specific evidence that would change your mind — a specific benchmark comparison, a specific stretch of underperformance, a specific number of years. If no evidence you can name would actually change the self-rating, that's a sign the rating isn't really a conclusion drawn from evidence at all, but a fixed piece of identity wearing evidence's clothing.

Revisit the comparison periodically rather than settling it once. A self-rating formed years ago, during a favorable stretch, can quietly outlive the conditions that produced it. Set a standing reminder to re-run the honest, documented comparison against a real benchmark at least once a year, rather than trusting a conclusion you reached once and have been carrying forward, unexamined, ever since.

In a group setting, ask everyone to write their self-rating down before anyone speaks. If you're ever part of a group exercise like the advisors' conference-room survey, notice what happens when self-ratings are gathered privately and in writing before being shared aloud, versus when they're offered casually in conversation. The written, private version tends to be more honest, since it removes the social pressure to match or exceed whatever confidence the room is already projecting.

Weight your best results and your worst results equally when forming a self-assessment. If you catch yourself building a case for your own above-average judgment out of a handful of standout decisions, deliberately locate an equal number of your worst decisions and give them the same weight in the final assessment. A fair, representative sample includes the picks you'd rather not think about, not only the ones you're proud to mention.

Half of any group is, by definition, below the median — and the fact that almost nobody in that half believes it's them is not evidence the math is wrong. It's evidence of exactly the bias this chapter is describing, operating on you as reliably as it operates on everyone else in the room.

Chapter 5 — The Near Miss That Felt Like Almost Winning

Why a Bet That Barely Failed Gets Remembered Like a Bet That Barely Succeeded

Two numbers away. That's how she describes it afterward, to anyone who asks and several people who don't — the lottery ticket that matched four of six numbers, missing the jackpot by two digits that, in her retelling, feel like they were agonizingly close, a hair's breadth from a life-changing outcome rather than what they mathematically were, which is exactly as far from winning as a ticket that matched none of the six numbers at all. She buys tickets more frequently in the weeks following that near-miss than she did before it, not because anything about the actual odds has changed, but because the near-miss produced a feeling distinctly different from an ordinary loss — a feeling closer to almost-winning than to simply losing, a feeling that seems to be telling her something true about how close she's getting, when in fact the lottery, structurally, doesn't have a "getting close" — every combination is exactly as unlikely as every other combination, and missing by two numbers carries precisely zero additional information about how the next ticket will perform.

Consider a version of the same mechanism with considerably more money attached. A day trader watching a position approach, but narrowly fail to reach, a specific price target he'd set in advance describes the trade afterward not as a loss but as something closer to a validation of his read — he was "right about the direction," the trade "almost worked," the setup was "basically correct" and simply needed slightly better timing on the exit. He increases his position size on the next similar setup, reasoning that a strategy this close to working consistently must be fundamentally sound, in need only of minor refinement rather than serious reconsideration. What this framing omits is that "almost reaching a price target" and "reaching a price target" are, for the purposes of the actual trade's profit and loss, entirely different outcomes with nothing meaningfully connecting them — the position that almost hit the target and the position that missed it entirely both simply didn't hit the target, and treating the near-miss as partial evidence of a correct read, rather than as the loss it actually was, systematically inflates his confidence in a strategy that hasn't actually demonstrated the reliability he's crediting it with.

A third scene shows the mechanism in a business context, where the stakes and the timelines are both considerably longer. An entrepreneur pitching investors for a second, larger round of funding describes a previous product launch that fell just short of its sales targets — reaching roughly ninety percent of the projected number — not as a disappointing shortfall but, in the pitch itself, as proof of "product-market fit that just needs more marketing spend to fully realize," a framing that treats a genuine miss as evidence pointing toward eventual success rather than as a signal that the underlying assumptions behind the original projection might have been meaningfully wrong. The framing works, in the sense that it secures the funding. Whether the underlying business logic supporting that framing was actually sound is a separate question the near-miss, on its own, provides very little real evidence about either way.

A fourth scene shows the mechanism operating in a domain with much longer feedback cycles than a lottery drawing or a trading screen. A job seeker who applies for a competitive, highly sought-after promotion within her company advances through three rounds of interviews before ultimately losing the position to another internal candidate by what her manager describes, in a debrief, as "an extremely close call." She spends the following months describing the process, to colleagues and to herself, not as a rejection but as something closer to a near-hire — proof, she tells herself, that she's genuinely ready for the next level and simply needs to wait for the right specific opening rather than reconsidering anything about her actual readiness or approach. When a second, different opportunity opens up four months later, she pursues it with the same approach and the same materials that produced the earlier near-miss, making no substantive changes, reasoning that a process this close to succeeding the first time barely needs adjusting — a reasoning the near-miss framing supports far more comfortably than an honest read of the actual feedback she received, some of which pointed to specific, addressable gaps she never fully absorbed because the "so close" framing of the first attempt left little room for hearing them as anything but formalities.

A fifth scene shows the mechanism operating at a much smaller, more frequent scale, worth including because it illustrates how routinely this pattern can recur without ever registering as significant. A recreational golfer whose putt lips out of the cup — circling the rim before rolling away rather than dropping in — describes the shot afterward as though it had gone in, mentally logging it alongside his actual makes when recalling his round to friends later that evening. Repeated across dozens of rounds over a season, this habit of counting near-makes alongside actual makes leaves him with a considerably inflated sense of his own putting statistics, a distortion with no real financial stakes in this specific context but built from the exact same cognitive machinery that, applied to a trading account instead of a golf green, produces the considerably more expensive versions of this pattern the rest of this chapter describes.

What's actually happening

The specific psychological mechanism operating in these scenes is well-documented in research on gambling behavior under the label of the near-miss effect, studied extensively by researchers including Robert Reid, whose foundational 1986 work established that outcomes falling just short of a win are processed by the brain in ways meaningfully different from — and considerably more encouraging than — outcomes that fail by a wide margin, even though both are, in any objective sense, equally complete losses. Reid's research and the substantial body of work that followed it found that near-misses generate physiological and behavioral responses more similar to actual wins than to ordinary losses, and that gamblers exposed to a higher proportion of near-misses persist longer and bet more than gamblers experiencing an equivalent number of losses without the near-miss framing — a finding so consistent and so exploitable that slot machine designers have been documented deliberately engineering reel outcomes to produce a higher-than-random rate of near-misses specifically because of the persistence effect this research established.

A neuroscientific layer, drawn from research conducted by neuroscientist Luke Clark and colleagues, adds to this picture — research which used brain imaging to examine how near-misses are processed relative to both wins and clear losses. Clark's research found that near-misses activate reward-related regions of the brain — including circuitry associated with the neurotransmitter dopamine, closely linked to motivation and the pursuit of future rewards — at levels considerably closer to an actual win's activation pattern than to a clear loss's, despite near-misses and clear losses being, in terms of actual monetary outcome, identical. This finding matters enormously for understanding why the near-miss effect is so resistant to purely rational correction: the brain isn't making a conscious, reasoned error in judgment that a person could simply think their way out of with better information. It's registering a genuinely different, more reward-adjacent physiological response to the near-miss itself, a response that occurs before, and largely independent of, any conscious evaluation of what actually happened.

Precisely why a near-miss produces this specific response, rather than being processed simply as an ordinary loss, matters here, and the leading explanation connects directly back to the earlier chapters in this book. A near-miss appears to activate the same skill-attribution machinery Chapter 1 described, but in a distorted, premature way: missing narrowly feels like evidence that the underlying approach was fundamentally correct, requiring only a small adjustment, which is a specific, flattering story about the near-miss that a wide miss doesn't offer nearly as readily. Losing badly is harder to reframe as "almost right." Losing narrowly is remarkably easy to reframe that way, and that ease of reframing is precisely what makes near-misses so much more encouraging, and so much more dangerous, than an equivalent clear loss.

A further mechanism, connected to research on counterfactual thinking — the mental process of imagining alternative outcomes that didn't actually happen. Psychologists studying counterfactual reasoning have found that outcomes which came close to a different, better result generate considerably more vivid, more emotionally charged mental simulations of that alternative outcome than outcomes that missed by a wide margin, a pattern that has been documented across contexts ranging from Olympic medal ceremonies — silver medalists, who came closer to gold, frequently report less satisfaction than bronze medalists, who narrowly avoided no medal at all — to everyday decision-making. Applied to a near-miss trade or a near-target sales quarter, this means the vivid, easily-imagined alternative universe where the bet succeeded gets weighted, emotionally, almost as heavily as if it had actually happened, coloring the person's read of the actual, real outcome with a borrowed optimism that the real result never earned.

One final piece connects this chapter back to Chapter 1's ledger mechanism directly: a near-miss is, structurally, an unusually easy loss to file under the flattering half of an uneven ledger, considerably easier than a clear, decisive loss would be. A clear loss requires some active reframing to externalize — inventing an excuse, blaming a factor outside your control. A near-miss barely requires any reframing at all, because the story it tells about itself — *I almost had it* — is already halfway to a flattering narrative before any conscious editing even begins. This is part of why the near-miss effect is so much stickier than an ordinary attribution error: the self-serving story isn't something the mind has to construct from scratch. It's something the near-miss hands over, nearly finished, the instant it happens.

One more piece from the gambling research literature specifically belongs here, because it clarifies why near-misses are so effective at sustaining engagement rather than simply feeling mildly encouraging. Researchers studying slot machine design have documented that machines can be, and often are, deliberately calibrated to deliver a higher rate of near-misses than pure chance alone would produce — arranging reel symbols so that a losing spin lands one position away from a jackpot far more often than random placement would predict. This isn't a marginal design detail. It's a core part of how these machines are engineered to keep players engaged, precisely because the near-miss effect this chapter describes is reliable and predictable enough to be exploited deliberately. The takeaway for financial decision-making is a sober one: if a near-miss effect this powerful is worth deliberately engineering into a gambling product, it's worth taking seriously as a genuine, reliable bias in your own financial judgment, not a minor quirk you can simply reason your way past once you've heard about it.

What it costs you

The most direct cost mirrors the hot-hand pattern from Chapter 3, applied to a single near-miss rather than a streak: a strategy, trade, or business approach that produced a narrow failure gets treated as functionally validated rather than functionally rejected, leading to a repeated or larger bet on the same approach without the kind of honest reconsideration a clear, unambiguous loss would have prompted. The day trader's increased position size on the next similar setup is funded, psychologically, by a near-miss the underlying math never actually supported as evidence of anything beyond an ordinary loss.

There's a second cost specific to how near-misses distort the evaluation of a business or a plan over a longer horizon. The entrepreneur's ninety-percent sales result, reframed as near-success rather than genuine shortfall, can lead to continued investment in an underlying approach whose actual weaknesses never get seriously examined, because the near-miss framing keeps the conversation focused on minor optimization — more marketing spend, slightly better execution — rather than on the harder, more useful question of whether the original assumptions behind the projection were meaningfully flawed to begin with.

A third cost is behavioral and compounds specifically in any context involving repeated, frequent bets — a slot machine, a trading strategy executed often, a sales cycle repeated quarter after quarter. Because near-misses generate a persistence-encouraging response nearly as strong as an actual win, a strategy or environment that reliably produces a high proportion of near-misses will keep a person engaged, and betting, considerably longer than the strategy's actual, honest win rate would otherwise justify — which is precisely why environments engineered to produce frequent near-misses are so much more costly, over time, than environments where losses simply look and feel like losses.

A fourth cost is specific to slower, longer-cycle domains like the job seeker's promotion pursuit: a near-miss can suppress genuinely useful, specific feedback from ever being absorbed, because the emotional framing of "so close" makes any critical detail in that feedback feel like a minor footnote rather than a real signal worth acting on. This is a particular kind of cost the trading and gambling examples don't fully capture — it isn't just that the near-miss inflates confidence about the next attempt. It's that the near-miss actively drowns out the most useful information available for improving that next attempt, precisely at the moment the information was most directly on offer.

A fifth cost accumulates specifically across a lifetime of small, low-stakes near-misses like the golfer's lipped putt: repeated over years, in a domain with genuinely low individual stakes, this pattern quietly trains a general habit of counting near-successes as successes that can migrate, largely unnoticed, into higher-stakes financial domains where the identical habit becomes considerably more expensive. The golfer's inflated sense of his own putting statistics costs him nothing financially. The identical mental habit, applied without adjustment to a trading account or a business pitch, costs considerably more, and the habit doesn't arrive labeled by domain — it's the same generalized tendency, practiced harmlessly in one part of a person's life and expensively in another.

How this shows up without you noticing

The clearest tell is the specific phrase "so close," used about an outcome that was, in every dollar-and-cents or pass-fail sense, a complete failure. Listen for it in your own retelling of a decision that didn't work — a trade that just missed a target, a deal that fell through at the last stage, a bid that lost by a narrow margin. The phrase feels descriptive, almost neutral. It's actually doing quiet persuasive work, nudging the listener, and the speaker, toward treating the miss as a near-success rather than the loss it structurally was.

The overrides

Score a near-miss exactly the way you'd score a clear loss, on paper, every time. In whatever record you're keeping of your decisions and outcomes, resist the urge to create a special, softer category for results that came close but didn't succeed. A miss is a miss, regardless of the margin, for the purposes of evaluating whether the underlying approach is actually working — treat it that way in your written record even when it doesn't feel that way emotionally.

Ask what specifically would need to change, concretely, before betting again on a near-miss's strategy. If a trade, plan, or approach fell just short, don't allow "it almost worked" to stand in for an actual, specific diagnosis. Name precisely what would need to be different for the same approach to succeed next time — and if you can't name anything specific and well-supported, treat the near-miss as evidence the approach doesn't yet work, not evidence that it nearly does.

Notice the vivid alternate-outcome feeling for what it is. If you catch yourself replaying, in detail, the version of events where a near-miss became a win, recognize that vivid replay as an emotional artifact of counterfactual thinking rather than as useful information about how likely that alternate outcome actually was. The vividness of an imagined alternative says nothing about its probability.

Be specifically wary of any environment or product engineered to produce frequent near-misses. Certain games, certain trading platforms with fast, frequent feedback, and certain sales structures are more likely than others to generate a high rate of narrow misses by design, precisely because near-misses keep people engaged longer than clear losses would. Recognizing when you're in this kind of environment is itself a useful piece of self-protection.

Separate "the direction was right" from "the trade was right." Being correct about a general direction — a stock was going to rise, a market was going to move a certain way — is a different, much weaker claim than having correctly timed and sized a specific bet on that direction. A near-miss often proves the first claim while disproving the second, and conflating them is exactly how a losing trade gets miscounted as a validating one.

Give critical feedback its own dedicated review, separate from the emotional aftermath of the near-miss. If you received specific, substantive feedback alongside a narrow loss — a hiring manager's notes, an investor's stated reasons for passing, a coach's specific critique — schedule a deliberate, calm re-read of that feedback a few days later, once the "so close" feeling has faded, rather than trusting your first-pass reading of it in the immediate emotional aftermath.

Log near-misses in the same place and the same format as clear losses. Keep near-misses in your written decision record exactly as you would a decisive loss, using identical language and identical detail, rather than giving them their own softer, more flattering entry. Reviewing the two side by side, later, makes the near-miss's actual severity considerably harder to minimize than memory alone would allow.

Watch for the phrase "almost" doing quiet persuasive work in your own low-stakes hobbies, too. Notice patterns like the golfer's lipped putt in your own recreational life — activities where near-misses get casually folded into your sense of your own success rate. Catching the habit somewhere low-stakes and harmless is good practice for noticing it before it operates, unexamined, somewhere considerably more expensive.

Ask what a truly random, unrelated near-miss would tell you, as a sanity check. Imagine an outcome that missed by the identical narrow margin but in a context you have no emotional stake in — a stranger's near-miss rather than your own. Would you consider that outcome meaningful evidence of anything?

Applying the same standard to your own near-miss, rather than a more generous one reserved for yourself, often reveals how little the margin itself actually proves.

A near-miss and a clear loss cost you the identical amount of money — the only difference between them is how convincingly one of them lies to you about what almost happened.

Chapter 6 — The Bigger Bet After the Win

How Confidence, Once Inflated, Gets Spent on the Very Next Decision

The first position was modest, sized the way a first position from someone genuinely uncertain about their own judgment should be sized — a small enough stake that a total loss would sting without threatening anything structural in the rest of his finances. It worked, and worked well, well enough that the second position, opened within days of closing the first, was more than double the size, funded partly by the actual proceeds of the win and partly by an appetite for risk that had visibly grown alongside the account balance. The second position also worked, though by a narrower margin, and the third — opened before the second had even fully closed, in a related but distinct instrument, sized larger still — did not. By the time he pauses to actually total the sequence, several weeks in, the loss on the third position alone is larger than the combined gains of the first two, a fact he finds genuinely surprising in the moment, because each individual step in the escalation had felt, at the time, like a reasonable, incremental adjustment rather than what the full sequence, laid out end to end, actually was: a rapid, compounding expansion of risk, funded almost entirely by the confidence two earlier, smaller wins had produced.

This chapter is where the earlier mechanisms in this book stop being abstract psychology and start showing up directly in position size, because everything discussed so far — the self-serving ledger, the illusion of control, the hot-hand belief, the sense of being better than average, the near-miss that felt like validation — ultimately expresses itself the same way, in the one place it actually costs money: a bet made larger than the last one, funded by confidence a genuinely honest accounting of the evidence would not fully support.

Consider a second, quieter version of the same escalation, playing out over months rather than weeks. A woman who began investing cautiously several years earlier, starting with small, diversified positions she checked infrequently, describes her current approach — considerably more concentrated, considerably more actively managed, considerably larger relative to her total savings than her original approach was — as the natural result of having "learned what works" over her several years of experience. Asked to actually trace the specific decisions that led from her original cautious approach to her current concentrated one, the honest sequence looks less like a gradual, well-reasoned evolution and more like a series of individually small escalations, each one following closely on the heels of a win, each one justified at the time by the win that preceded it, none of them independently reconsidered against her original, more cautious reasoning for diversifying in the first place. The escalation, examined honestly, wasn't really driven by years of accumulated wisdom. It was driven by a sequence of individual wins, each one funding a slightly larger bet on the theory that the growing string of successes justified it.

A third scene shows the escalation compressed into a much shorter timeframe than either of the two above, which makes the pattern easier to see in full. A cryptocurrency trader, new to the asset class, turns a small initial stake into a considerably larger sum across a single volatile week, riding a handful of favorable price swings with progressively larger position sizes each time, funded almost entirely by the previous swing's proceeds. By the fifth trade of the week, he's risking an amount that would have seemed unthinkable to him on the first day, justified in the moment by a felt sense that he's "figured out the rhythm" of this particular market — a rhythm that, on the sixth trade, fails to repeat, wiping out the majority of the week's accumulated gains along with a meaningful portion of his original stake in a single afternoon. Asked afterward how he arrived at the size of that sixth trade, he struggles to reconstruct a specific, reasoned answer beyond "it felt like the natural next step" — a natural next step that only makes sense as an extension of the five trades immediately before it, not as an independently justified decision on its own terms.

A fourth scene shows the same escalation playing out in a context with no trading screen at all: a small-business owner who, after landing an unusually large single contract, immediately commits to a considerably larger lease on new commercial space, reasoning that a business capable of landing a contract that size clearly needs — and can clearly support — meaningfully more capacity going forward. The single contract, examined honestly a year later, turns out to have been an unusual, one-time opportunity rather than the leading edge of a durable new normal, and the expanded lease, signed in the immediate afterglow of the win, becomes a fixed monthly cost the business's more typical revenue struggles to comfortably support for the next three years of the agreement.

What's actually happening

The direct, empirical evidence for this pattern comes substantially from research conducted by economists Brad Barber and Terrance Odean, whose extensive body of work analyzing real brokerage account data — introduced in Chapter 4's discussion of overplacement — documents this escalation dynamic in specific, quantified detail. Their research, including work published under titles as directly relevant as "Trading Is Hazardous to Your Wealth," found that individual investors who experience gains tend to increase their subsequent trading activity and risk-taking measurably more than the underlying evidence about their own skill would justify, and that this increased activity, on average, correlates with reduced net returns once transaction costs are properly accounted for. The pattern isn't limited to any one type of investor or account size — it appears across a wide range of individual investors, with the magnitude of the effect correlating with independently measured levels of investor overconfidence, exactly as this book's earlier chapters would predict.

A specific behavioral-finance concept applies directly here, because it captures precisely what's happening in both scenes above: the disposition to treat gains as evidence supporting expanded risk-taking is closely related to, though distinct from, the house-money effect discussed at length in this library's companion volume on windfalls — the tendency to treat winnings as less "real" and therefore more available for looser risk-taking than an original stake. What this chapter is describing is a related but separate mechanism: it isn't only that the winnings themselves feel less real and get risked more loosely. It's that the win, independent of what happens to the specific winnings, updates the investor's belief about their own skill level, and that updated, inflated belief then gets applied to the entire portfolio going forward — including money that has nothing to do with the original win at all. The man in this chapter's opening scene didn't just risk his winnings more loosely. He risked his entire subsequent decision-making more aggressively, funded by a confidence increase the single win, honestly evaluated, didn't actually earn.

This connects directly back to the self-serving attribution mechanism from Chapter 1, because the two combine in a specific, mutually reinforcing way that explains why the escalation tends to accelerate rather than proceed at a steady pace. Each win gets filed as evidence of skill, per Chapter 1's mechanism. That inflated sense of skill increases confidence, which increases the size of the next bet, per this chapter's mechanism. If the next, larger bet also succeeds — which happens often enough, purely by chance, to keep the cycle going — the larger win gets filed as even stronger evidence of skill, because a larger, more consequential-feeling win produces a more vivid, more convincing story than a small one did. This creates a genuine feedback loop, not a simple linear progression: confidence and bet size can escalate together at an accelerating rate, each reinforcing the other, right up until a loss large enough to break the cycle finally arrives — a loss that, by the time it does arrive, is sized considerably larger than any of the wins that built the confidence funding it.

A related finding from research on regret and decision-making under risk connects this chapter to the broader literature on how prior outcomes shape subsequent risk tolerance. Studies examining risk-taking following a prior gain versus a prior loss have consistently found that a recent gain measurably increases willingness to take on additional risk in a subsequent, unrelated decision — a pattern documented across both laboratory experiments and real financial decision-making, and one that appears to operate largely independent of whether the increased risk is actually justified by any new information about the specific opportunity being considered. The mechanism isn't limited to financial windfalls narrowly defined — any recent positive outcome appears capable of producing a measurable increase in subsequent risk appetite, which is precisely why the pattern this chapter describes shows up not just after a large financial win but after any sequence of decisions that felt, subjectively, like a run of success.

A further, specific finding, directly relevant to the cryptocurrency trader's story, describes how quickly this escalation can compress in fast-moving markets. Research on trading behavior in high-volatility, rapid-feedback environments has found that the confidence-building effect of a win appears to strengthen, not weaken, when the feedback arrives quickly and repeatedly — a fast sequence of wins compresses the entire escalation dynamic this chapter describes into a much shorter window than a sequence of wins spread across months or years would produce, giving the trader far less real time to notice the pattern building before the position sizes involved have already grown large enough to matter. Slower markets give overconfidence more time to be caught. Faster ones don't.

One more piece connects this chapter's mechanism to the neuroscience of reward processing more broadly. Research on how the brain's dopamine system responds to rewards has found that unpredictable, variable rewards — the exact shape a sequence of wins and losses in an active trading account takes — produce a stronger, more persistent motivational response than predictable, steady rewards of equivalent average value. This helps explain why an escalating sequence of trades can feel considerably more compelling, moment to moment, than a slower, steadier approach to the identical underlying opportunity, even when the steadier approach would likely produce better risk-adjusted results over time. The brain isn't simply responding to the money. It's responding to the specific, variable pattern of wins and losses, which is precisely the pattern an escalating sequence of increasingly large bets reliably produces.

What it costs you

The most direct cost is exactly the arithmetic visible in this chapter's opening scene: because bet size tends to grow across a winning sequence, the eventual loss that ends the sequence — and some loss, eventually, virtually always arrives, since no genuine or illusory edge survives an unlimited escalation in size forever — tends to be considerably larger than the sum of the gains that preceded it. This produces a specific, brutal asymmetry that shows up again and again in real trading and investing histories: a long sequence of modest, individually satisfying wins, followed by one loss large enough to erase all of them and more, a pattern researchers studying trading behavior have documented repeatedly across both professional and individual investor accounts.

There's a second cost that compounds beyond any single sequence: an investor whose bet sizing is driven substantially by recent outcomes rather than by a consistent, independently reasoned risk framework never actually develops or tests a stable approach to position sizing at all. Every sizing decision becomes a referendum on how the last few decisions happened to go, rather than an application of any durable principle — which means the investor's risk exposure at any given moment says more about their recent luck than about any considered assessment of the actual opportunity or their actual capacity to absorb a loss.

A third cost, less visible than the financial one, shows up in the psychological aftermath of the eventual large loss that ends an escalating sequence. Because the escalation was funded by a belief in a personal skill level the honest evidence never fully supported, the eventual correction — the loss large enough to force a reassessment — tends to land not just as a financial setback but as a genuine identity crisis, precisely because so much personal narrative had been built, across the winning sequence, around the idea that the wins reflected something durable and real about the person's own judgment. Unwinding that narrative, once the loss arrives, is considerably harder than it would have been to simply size the bets more conservatively throughout.

A fourth cost, specific to fast-moving markets like the one in the cryptocurrency scene, is the sheer compression of the entire cycle — confidence building, size escalating, and the eventual correction arriving — into a timeframe too short for the ordinary correctives this book recommends, like a quarterly review or a cooling-off period, to naturally intervene before the damage is done. This makes fast markets a specific, higher-risk environment for this chapter's pattern, one that calls for tighter, more automatic sizing rules precisely because there's less real time available for a person's own judgment to catch the escalation in progress.

A fifth cost is specific to the business-expansion version of this pattern illustrated by the leased commercial space: unlike a trading position, a fixed cost taken on in the immediate aftermath of a single large win cannot simply be closed out the moment conditions revert to normal. It persists, as a monthly obligation, for the full length of whatever commitment was signed, which means the escalation cost in these slower-moving domains isn't a single large loss absorbed once — it's a recurring, compounding drag that continues to be paid, month after month, long after the confidence that justified it has quietly faded.

How this shows up without you noticing

Watch for a specific pattern in how a position size gets described: "I figured I'd let it ride" or "I put more behind it this time since it's already working." Notice that this language treats the previous win as though it were information about the next bet's odds, when in most of the situations this book covers, it isn't. The tell isn't the size increase itself — sometimes a larger position really is justified by genuinely new information. The tell is whether the stated reason for the increase is the previous outcome itself, rather than anything new learned about the specific opportunity in front of you right now.

The overrides

Set a maximum sizing rule before any winning streak begins, and hold it regardless of recent results. Decide, in a calm moment with no active streak influencing your judgment, what the largest single position or bet you're willing to make actually is, as a fixed rule rather than a feeling — and hold that ceiling regardless of how many consecutive wins precede the next decision. The entire value of this rule comes from setting it before the streak starts, since you will not reliably set a sensible ceiling in the middle of one.

Require a cooling-off period before any position size increase, proportional to how large the increase is. The larger the proposed jump in bet size relative to your previous typical size, the longer the mandatory pause you commit to before acting on it — a rule that specifically targets the accelerating feedback loop this chapter describes, by inserting deliberate friction exactly where the pattern tends to accelerate fastest.

Separate the decision to reinvest winnings from the decision to increase overall risk exposure. These are two different choices that tend to get bundled together without examination. You can choose to keep winnings invested without simultaneously choosing to take on a larger, more concentrated, or more aggressive overall risk posture — treating them as separate decisions, made independently, breaks the automatic link between a recent win and an expanded appetite for the next one.

Track your position sizing against your win streak explicitly, in writing. Keep a simple running record of your position sizes alongside your recent outcomes. If you notice size climbing in step with a recent string of wins, without any specific new information justifying the increase, that correlation alone is worth treating as a warning sign rather than as evidence of well-earned, growing confidence.

Ask what size you'd choose if you'd just experienced the opposite outcome. Before increasing a bet, imagine that your most recent result had actually been a loss rather than a win, and ask what size you'd be considering under that counterfactual. If the honest answer is meaningfully smaller, the size you're actually about to commit to is being driven by the recent outcome rather than by the underlying merits of the specific decision in front of you.

Set an explicit "pause and reassess" trigger tied to cumulative gains, not just individual wins. Beyond a single-position size cap, set a rule for your overall account: if total gains from a recent stretch cross a specific threshold, pause all new position sizing decisions for a defined period and conduct a full, honest review before continuing. This targets the accelerating feedback loop directly, at the account level rather than the individual-trade level, where it's often hardest to notice from inside any single decision.

Treat a fast, compressed sequence of wins with extra suspicion, not extra confidence. If a string of favorable outcomes has arrived unusually quickly — within days rather than months — apply a stricter, not looser, sizing rule to whatever comes next, since a compressed timeframe gives you less real opportunity to notice the pattern building before the position sizes involved have already grown large.

For fixed, hard-to-reverse commitments like a lease or a hire, apply a separate, longer cooling-off period than you would for a liquid position. Because a structural commitment can't be unwound the way a trading position can, hold expansion decisions made in the immediate aftermath of an unusually large win to a stricter standard than an equivalent decision made from a slower, steadier baseline — the reversibility of a decision should directly shape how much scrutiny it receives before being made.

Keep a visible running total of cumulative risk taken across a sequence, not just the size of the most recent bet. A single position that looks reasonable in isolation can be part of a sequence that, added together, represents a considerably larger and more concentrated risk than any individual decision within it would suggest. Track the running total explicitly, somewhere you'll actually see it, rather than evaluating each new bet only against the one immediately before it.

Give yourself permission, in advance, to walk away from a winning streak entirely. Decide, while calm, that there is no rule requiring you to keep playing a sequence simply because it's currently going well. Stopping voluntarily at a self-chosen point, rather than only stopping once a loss forces the issue, is one of the few moves in this entire chapter that costs nothing to execute and removes the escalation risk completely for as long as you hold to it.

The size of your next bet should be justified by the specific evidence for that specific bet — not by how good the last one felt. A winning streak funds confidence far more reliably than it funds an actual edge, and only one of those two things should be setting your position size.

Chapter 7 — The Story That Makes the Loss Someone Else's Fault

Why the Explanation for a Bad Outcome Rarely Points Back at the Decision Itself

The position lost money, and by the time he's finished explaining it to his brother-in-law over dinner, the loss has acquired a full cast of external culprits: a piece of unexpected regulatory news nobody could have anticipated, a broader market downturn that dragged down even fundamentally sound positions, and — delivered almost as an aside — a vague reference to "the algorithms" distorting short-term price action in ways that make the market harder to read fairly than it used to be. Nowhere in the explanation does the actual decision itself come up as a candidate cause — the sizing, the entry timing, the fact that the position was concentrated well beyond what his own stated risk tolerance from a year earlier would have permitted. The loss happened to him, in the story he's telling. It wasn't produced by a specific, examinable choice he made.

This chapter looks directly at what happens after the loss that every earlier chapter in this book has been building toward —

the moment the escalating confidence finally meets a result large enough to threaten it, and the specific, well-documented ways the story of that loss gets rewritten to protect the confidence rather than to correct it.

Consider a second version of the same instinct, playing out with a longer memory attached. A woman reviewing her investment decisions from several years earlier, now that the outcomes are fully known, describes a specific bad call — a concentrated bet in a sector that subsequently underperformed for years — as something she "couldn't have known" would go badly, a framing that treats the decision as having been reasonable given the information available at the time. Pressed gently by a friend who remembers the actual conversation from years earlier, it emerges that the friend had specifically raised a concern about the concentration at the time, a concern the woman had waved off in the moment with more confidence than the situation, in hindsight, actually warranted. The story she's telling now — that nobody could have known — isn't simply false. It's a specific, subtle distortion: someone did raise exactly the concern that turned out to matter, at the time it would have mattered, and the story has quietly edited that inconvenient fact out of the record in favor of a version where the loss was genuinely unforeseeable rather than a risk she'd been specifically warned about and chose to accept anyway.

A third scene shows the mechanism operating in a family financial decision rather than an individual investing one. A couple who jointly decided to co-sign a substantial loan for a sibling's business venture, against the quiet reservations of one of the two partners, watches the venture fail within two years, leaving them responsible for a debt they hadn't planned around. In the retelling that becomes the couple's settled version of events over the following months, the failure gets attributed almost entirely to the sibling's poor execution and to a market downturn that hit the sibling's specific industry — both genuinely real factors, worth naming honestly. What the retelling omits, consistently, is the couple's own decision to co-sign in the first place, made with considerably less due diligence than a loan of that size would ordinarily receive, and made partly on the strength of the more confident partner's insistence that the sibling's plan was "obviously going to work."

The specific decision to co-sign, the one piece of the story that was actually theirs to control, never gets examined with anything like the scrutiny applied to the sibling's execution or the industry's downturn — both real contributors, and both considerably easier to discuss than the couple's own underwriting judgment.

A fourth scene shows a milder, more everyday version of the same instinct. A man who consistently overpacks his suitcase for every trip, despite repeated experience suggesting he never uses most of what he brings, attributes a specific instance of arriving with an overweight-baggage fee not to his own packing habits but to "the airline changing its weight limits without properly announcing it" — a claim he hasn't actually verified and that turns out, on checking, to be false; the limit hadn't changed at all. The stakes here are trivial compared to the rest of this chapter's scenes, but the shape of the reasoning is identical: a specific, checkable external cause gets reached for and accepted without verification, precisely because it's more comfortable than examining a personal habit that's produced the identical result on more than one previous occasion.

A fifth scene closes this chapter's opening with a workplace version of the pattern, useful because it shows how outcome bias can operate on an entire team's shared institutional memory rather than a single person's private story. A sales team that missed its quarterly target after a senior member pushed through an unusually aggressive pricing change over the objections of two colleagues holds a retrospective meeting in which the missed target gets attributed, in the official summary that circulates afterward, to "a softer-than-expected market" — a real factor, but one that the two colleagues who'd raised specific concerns about the pricing change beforehand recognize immediately as an incomplete account. Neither colleague corrects the summary in the meeting itself, since doing so would mean directly contradicting a senior team member in front of the group, and the incomplete version becomes the team's official, permanent record of what happened that quarter, available to be cited, uncorrected, the next time a similar pricing decision comes up for discussion.

What's actually happening

The mechanism operating in these scenes connects directly to research on what's called outcome bias, studied extensively by psychologists Jonathan Baron and John Hershey in a foundational 1988 paper. Baron and Hershey demonstrated that people systematically evaluate the quality of a past decision based substantially on how it turned out, rather than on how reasonable the decision actually was given the information available at the time it was made — a subtle but important distinction, since a genuinely good decision can produce a bad outcome purely through bad luck, and a genuinely bad decision can produce a good outcome purely through good luck. What Baron and Hershey's research showed specifically is that people don't just apply this outcome-based evaluation evenhandedly to decisions in general — they apply it asymmetrically to their own decisions in a way that protects their self-image, which connects directly back to the self-serving attribution mechanism from Chapter 1: a bad outcome from your own decision gets explained away as bad luck rather than a bad decision, while — in a related but distinct pattern — a bad outcome from someone else's decision, or a decision you're evaluating with less personal investment, is much more readily judged as having reflected poor judgment in the first place.

This connects directly to Baruch Fischhoff's hindsight bias research, introduced briefly in Chapter 1, in a specific and important way for this chapter's subject: hindsight bias doesn't only operate on wins, making a lucky success feel like it was foreseeable skill all along. It operates just as powerfully, in the opposite direction, on losses that were genuinely preceded by a specific warning sign — the way the friend's concern about concentration got edited out of the woman's retold story. Fischhoff's research demonstrated that once an outcome is known, people don't just overestimate how predictable that outcome was in general — they also tend to selectively remember or forget specific pieces of prior information depending on whether those pieces support or complicate the story they'd prefer to tell about the decision now. A specific warning that turned out to be right becomes strangely hard to recall clearly; a specific reassurance that turned out to be wrong gets remembered as more reasonable and mainstream at the time than it actually was.

A further mechanism, connected to cognitive dissonance theory, first developed by psychologist Leon Festinger and extensively studied since, belongs in this picture. Festinger's foundational research established that people experience genuine psychological discomfort when holding two contradictory beliefs simultaneously — in this case, "I am someone who makes sound financial decisions" and "I made a decision that produced a bad outcome" — and that this discomfort creates real motivational pressure to resolve the contradiction, typically by adjusting whichever belief is easier to adjust rather than the one that's actually more accurate. Because the belief "I am someone who makes sound decisions" is generally more central to a person's broader self-concept and therefore more resistant to revision, the pressure of cognitive dissonance tends to get resolved instead by adjusting the story around the specific decision — reframing it as reasonable-given-the-information-available, or attributing the bad outcome to factors outside the decision itself — leaving the broader, more comfortable self-image intact.

A related and important finding from research on financial regret specifically belongs here, because it explains why this pattern is particularly strong in investing and trading compared to some other domains. Studies of investor psychology have found that people experience considerably more intense regret over losses that resulted from an active decision — buying, selling, or changing a position — than over equivalent losses that resulted from inaction, a pattern researchers have termed the omission-commission distinction in regret. This asymmetry creates a specific incentive, operating beneath conscious awareness, to construct explanations that make an active, regretted decision feel less like a genuine choice and more like something that happened to the person — external, unpredictable, imposed by circumstances — precisely because that reframing reduces the more intense regret associated with owning an active decision that went wrong.

One final piece connects this chapter's mechanism directly to the co-signing couple's story: outcome bias operates with particular force in decisions made jointly with another person, because the story that emerges afterward isn't shaped by one person's memory alone — it's negotiated, often unconsciously, between two people who each have their own stake in how the shared history gets told. In a couple where one partner pushed harder for a decision that went badly, the collectively agreed-upon retelling frequently ends up externalizing the cause more heavily than either partner's private, honest assessment would on its own, because a shared story that avoids assigning blame to either partner is, in the moment, considerably more comfortable to live inside than a shared story that names a specific misjudgment and asks who made it.

A further, useful distinction from decision-theory research — between a good decision and a good outcome — runs through everything Baron and Hershey's work established. A decision can be genuinely well-reasoned, given the information honestly available at the time, and still produce a bad result purely through chance — and a decision can be genuinely careless, made on a hunch with no real diligence behind it, and still produce a good result purely through luck. Outcome bias collapses this distinction in both directions, but its cost is asymmetric: crediting a careless decision that happened to work out doesn't just fail to punish the carelessness — per Chapter 1's mechanism, it actively reinforces it, teaching the decision-maker that the careless approach is validated, precisely the setup for a considerably more expensive version of the identical carelessness the next time the stakes are higher.

What it costs you

The most direct and important cost, connecting back to the broader argument of this book, is that a loss whose story has been rewritten to externalize its cause never actually gets diagnosed correctly, which means the specific decision-making error that produced it — sizing too large, ignoring a legitimate warning, entering on a hunch rather than a genuinely researched read — survives fully intact and available to be repeated. The woman who edited her friend's warning out of her own retold story hasn't just protected her self-image. She's actively degraded her own ability to recognize a similar warning sign the next time one arrives, because the mental record she's working from no longer contains an accurate account of what actually happened the last time.

There's a second cost specific to relationships involving shared or observed financial decision-making. A person whose account of their own losses reliably externalizes blame, particularly when the externalizing involves editing out a specific concern someone else genuinely raised at the time, erodes that other person's confidence in future warnings being heard or taken seriously — why raise a concern again if it's simply going to be waved off in the moment and then erased from the story afterward. This can produce a specific, costly silence in exactly the relationships that could otherwise catch a mistake before it happens a second time.

A third cost compounds over a longer career or investing history: a person who never accurately diagnoses their own losses accumulates a track record whose actual lessons remain permanently unavailable to them, no matter how many individual losses they experience. Experience, in any genuinely skill-based domain, only produces real improvement when the feedback from each attempt gets processed honestly. A pattern of externalizing every loss's cause means the same number of years of "experience" produces considerably less actual learning than an honest observer, tracking the same history, would expect it to.

A fourth cost, illustrated clearly by the co-signing couple, shows up specifically in shared financial decisions where the actual, controllable decision — whether to co-sign, whether to invest jointly, whether to extend credit to a family member — gets buried beneath the more discussable, less personally implicating factors surrounding it. This means the one lesson most worth learning from the experience, about how the couple evaluates and vets a shared financial commitment before making it, is precisely the lesson their retold story is least equipped to teach them, since that lesson requires examining the one part of the story neither partner wants to revisit closely.

A fifth cost is a compounding one, worth naming because it explains why this pattern tends to get worse rather than better over a long financial life: each externalized loss makes the next externalization easier, because the person has now practiced, and reinforced, a specific narrative habit — the reflex of reaching for an external cause first, before ever seriously considering the decision itself. Like any practiced habit, it gets faster and more automatic with repetition, which means a person's tenth externalized loss requires considerably less conscious effort to construct than their first one did, precisely the opposite direction a genuinely self-correcting decision-maker's habits should be moving.

How this shows up without you noticing

Listen for the specific grammatical shift from active to passive voice around a loss. "I bought a large position in a stock that missed earnings" is active — it names a decision and an actor. "A position I was in got hit by a bad earnings miss" is passive — it turns the same event into something that happened to the speaker rather than something the speaker did. This shift often happens without any conscious intent to mislead, but it's worth noticing in your own language specifically, because the grammar of a retold loss frequently reveals the externalizing this chapter describes well before the content of the story does.

The overrides

Write down your reasoning and any concerns raised, by anyone, before the outcome is known. This override, first introduced in Chapter 1, matters even more specifically for this chapter's subject: a contemporaneous written record of any warning or concern raised about a decision — by you or by someone else — is close to the only reliable defense against a later, self-protective rewrite of what actually happened and who said what, when it mattered.

After any loss, explicitly separate the outcome from the decision quality, in both directions. Ask honestly: given only the information available at the time, was this actually a reasonable decision that happened to produce a bad result, or was it a poor decision that happened to get unlucky on top of already being poor? These require genuinely different responses — the first needs no real correction beyond accepting bad luck as a normal cost of taking any risk at all; the second needs an honest look at what specifically went wrong in the reasoning, not just the outcome.

Revisit any warning you dismissed, specifically, after the fact. If a loss occurred following a decision where someone — a partner, an advisor, a friend, your own earlier, more cautious self — raised a specific concern you chose to override, go back to that specific concern deliberately rather than letting it fade from the story. Ask honestly whether the concern was reasonable given what was actually known at the time, independent of how things turned out.

Notice the specific language of externalization and treat it as a flag rather than an explanation. Phrases like "nobody could have known," "the market did something nobody expected," or references to vague, unnamed external forces are worth pausing on specifically. Sometimes they're accurate. Often, on closer honest examination, they're doing exactly the protective work this chapter describes — treat the phrase itself as a prompt to look more closely rather than as a completed explanation.

Ask what you'd conclude about someone else who made the identical decision. If a friend or colleague described making the exact same decision, with the exact same information, and it produced the exact same loss, what would you honestly conclude about the quality of their decision-making? Applying that same standard to your own decision, rather than a more generous one reserved specifically for yourself, is often the fastest way to see past your own protective framing.

Give the concern you overrode its own line in your written record, permanently. If someone raised a specific concern you didn't act on and the concern turned out to matter, don't let that fact quietly disappear from your own account of what happened. Recording it honestly, even though it's uncomfortable, is what keeps the next similar warning from being dismissed just as easily.

Watch your own grammar around a loss. Notice whether you describe a loss using active language — "I bought," "I sized this too large," "I ignored a concern" — or passive language that turns the decision into something that simply happened to you. The shift from active to passive voice is often the first, quietest sign that a loss's story is beginning to drift away from an accurate account of what you actually did.

If a decision was made jointly, name the individual reasoning separately before agreeing on a shared story. In a couple, a partnership, or any shared financial decision, have each person independently write down their own honest account of what happened before negotiating a single, shared version. This slows down the tendency for a jointly-agreed story to quietly externalize blame more than either person's private, honest account would on its own.

Separate the question of blame from the question of diagnosis. A useful post-loss review isn't about assigning fault for its own sake, and framing it that way often triggers exactly the defensive externalizing this chapter describes. Reframe the exercise instead as pure diagnosis — not "whose fault was this" but "what specifically would need to be different for this not to happen again" — a question people find considerably easier to answer honestly, precisely because it doesn't require anyone to accept blame in order to participate in it usefully.

In a team or group setting, invite the quietest dissenting voice to speak first during any post-loss review. The colleague who raised the original concern is often the last person willing to bring it up again once a comfortable, externalized explanation has started circulating. Deliberately asking that specific person to speak first, before the group's preferred narrative has a chance to harden, meaningfully increases the odds that an accurate account survives into the team's permanent record of what happened.

A loss whose story blames everything except the decision that produced it isn't actually explained — it's just protected. And a decision that's protected instead of examined is a decision you will, with near certainty, eventually make again.

Chapter 8 — The Expert Who Stopped Checking

How Believing You've Already Arrived Makes You Stop Looking for Evidence You're Wrong

Ten years into managing his own portfolio, he's stopped reading the annual disclosures he used to read carefully in his first few years, stopped comparing his results against a benchmark the way he once did religiously every quarter, stopped seeking out perspectives that might challenge his current approach. None of this feels, to him, like carelessness. It feels like the natural, earned confidence of a decade of experience — he's put in the time, learned the lessons, developed an instinct he trusts, and checking every decision the way a beginner would seems, at this point, like an unnecessary formality for someone who's already demonstrated, through a decade of results, that he knows what he's doing. What this framing quietly skips over is a specific, uncomfortable question he hasn't actually asked in years: whether his results, honestly and completely tallied rather than remembered through the asymmetric ledger Chapter 1 described, actually support the level of confidence he's built, or whether the confidence has simply grown on its own, independent of the evidence, precisely because he stopped checking closely enough to notice if the two had quietly come apart.

Consider a second version of this pattern in a domain where the stakes of not-checking are more immediately visible. A financial advisor early in her career reviewed every recommendation she made against a documented checklist, sought a second opinion from a senior colleague on anything sizable, and tracked her own recommendations' outcomes meticulously against a benchmark, treating every discrepancy as something worth understanding. A decade into a genuinely successful career, with a strong reputation and a growing client base built substantially on real skill and real client outcomes, she's quietly stopped most of these practices — not through any single decision to abandon them, but through a gradual erosion, each step of which felt reasonable given how sound her instincts had proven to be. She would describe herself, accurately in most respects, as considerably more skilled now than she was a decade ago. What she'd have more trouble acknowledging is that the specific checking behaviors she's stopped doing were not incidental to that skill — they were part of what built it, and part of what would have caught the specific mistakes a genuinely confident, experienced professional is now more prone to make precisely because nobody, including herself, is checking her work as closely as they once did.

A third scene shows the same erosion happening to an entire small organization rather than a single individual. A three-person investment partnership that built its early success on a genuinely rigorous internal process — every position debated by all three partners before approval, every quarter reviewed against a written thesis for each holding — gradually lets that process slide as the fund's early returns build a strong, well-earned reputation among the partners themselves. New positions increasingly get approved on the strength of one partner's individual conviction, without the full debate the earlier process required, justified informally as an efficiency gained from years of working well together and trusting each other's judgment. The efficiency is real. What's quietly lost alongside it is the specific function the original, more cumbersome process served: catching an individual partner's blind spot before it became a position, a function that depended on the friction of dissent the newer, faster approach has mostly eliminated in the name of a trust the partnership's own early success helped build.

A fourth scene shows the same drift happening to a single household's ordinary financial habits rather than a professional practice. A couple who, in their first years of marriage, reviewed their combined spending together every month, reconciling every account and discussing every unusual expense, gradually let that monthly ritual lapse over a decade of generally stable, comfortable finances, reasoning informally that they'd clearly "figured out" how to manage money together and no longer needed the formal check-in. A modest but persistent billing error on a recurring subscription neither of them uses anymore goes unnoticed for over three years, quietly draining a small but real sum each month, precisely the kind of detail the abandoned monthly review would once have caught within weeks rather than years.

A fifth scene shows the pattern operating on a single decision-maker at the height of a genuinely distinguished career, worth including because it demonstrates that this pattern doesn't spare even the most objectively accomplished practitioners. A veteran portfolio manager with a multi-decade track record widely respected within her firm stops requiring her own junior analysts to formally challenge her larger position decisions, a step she'd insisted on for the first fifteen years of her career specifically because she'd seen how easily even skilled managers could miss an obvious flaw in their own reasoning. By her final years managing the fund before retirement, junior staff describe her decision process as "basically final" the moment she's expressed a preference, a shift she herself attributes to having simply gotten better at the job rather than to the specific loss of the structured challenge that had, for most of her career, been part of what made her good at it in the first place.

What's actually happening

The mechanism operating in these scenes connects to one of the more widely discussed, and frequently oversimplified, findings in psychology: the Dunning-Kruger effect, first documented by psychologists Justin Kruger and David Dunning in a 1999 paper that found people with genuinely low competence in a given skill area tend to significantly overestimate their own ability relative to others, in part because the same skills required to perform well in a domain are also the skills required to accurately judge performance in that domain — meaning a genuine lack of skill can produce a genuine inability to recognize that lack, a specific double bind Kruger and Dunning documented across several different task domains. It's worth being careful about how this finding gets applied here, because the popular version of the Dunning-Kruger effect has been considerably oversimplified and, in some cases, outright misrepresented in years since its publication — the original research specifically concerned people with genuinely low skill overestimating themselves, not a simple claim that confidence generally declines as competence rises, which later reanalyses have suggested is a much weaker and more contested pattern than popular summaries often present it as being.

What's genuinely useful and well-supported from this research, applied honestly to this chapter's subject, is narrower and more specific than the popularized version: competence in evaluating your own performance is itself a skill, separate from performance itself, and that evaluative skill can plateau or even erode over time in ways that aren't automatically corrected simply by accumulating more years of experience in the underlying activity. The financial advisor's decade of real, genuine skill growth in making client recommendations did not automatically come bundled with a proportional growth in her skill at accurately auditing her own recent decisions — those are related but genuinely distinct competencies, and the specific checking behaviors she abandoned were precisely the mechanism that had been substituting for, and partially compensating for, whatever gap existed between her actual skill and her self-assessment of it.

A related and important finding from research on positive illusions, conducted by psychologists Shelley Taylor and Jonathon Brown, belongs here too — research whose influential work found that mildly inflated, unrealistically positive self-perceptions are actually the psychological norm for most well-adjusted people, associated in their research with a range of generally positive outcomes including resilience and motivation — a genuinely more complicated and nuanced finding than a simple claim that all self-flattering illusion is harmful. Taylor and Brown's broader body of work is worth citing honestly here because it complicates a purely negative reading of overconfidence: some degree of positive illusion appears to serve a genuinely useful psychological function in many domains of life, and this book has no interest in claiming otherwise. What their research and subsequent work in this tradition also finds, however, is that the domains where mild positive illusion serves a person well tend to be domains with softer, more forgiving feedback and lower direct financial stakes — and that in domains involving concrete, quantifiable, high-stakes financial decisions specifically, the same illusions that might be harmless or even helpful in a person's general self-regard become measurably costly, because the feedback in financial markets, unlike much of ordinary social life, eventually arrives in a form — a number in an account — that doesn't bend to accommodate a flattering personal narrative the way social feedback often does.

A further mechanism, connected to research on feedback-seeking behavior more broadly, matters here: studies of professional development and skill acquisition across a range of fields have found that active, deliberate feedback-seeking — asking for critique, actively comparing your own performance against an objective standard, seeking out perspectives likely to disagree with you — tends to decline measurably as a person's perceived status or expertise within a field increases, even in fields where the actual, objective difficulty of continuing to improve hasn't decreased at all. This decline appears to be driven substantially by social and psychological factors rather than by any genuine reduction in how useful the feedback would be: asking for critique starts to feel, to an established, respected practitioner, like an admission of insufficient expertise, a specific social cost that a genuine beginner doesn't experience nearly as acutely, since a beginner asking for feedback is simply behaving as expected. The result is a specific, well-documented irony: feedback-seeking, which is often most valuable precisely at the point where a person's confidence and stakes have both grown largest, tends to decline exactly when it would be most useful to increase.

A further piece, connected directly to the partnership scene above, fits here: research on group decision-making has found that the presence of structured, required dissent — a formal devil's-advocate role, a mandatory second opinion, a documented debate before approval — meaningfully improves decision quality specifically in groups with a strong track record of prior success, precisely because prior success is exactly the condition under which informal, voluntary dissent becomes least likely to occur on its own. A group that has never had a major win has little standing confidence to protect and little social cost attached to voicing disagreement. A group with a genuinely strong track record has both, in abundance, which is why the structure needs to be built in deliberately rather than trusted to arise naturally out of a team's good working relationship.

A final, honest caveat belongs here, since this chapter's subject sits close to a genuinely difficult practical question: how much checking is actually enough, and when does additional checking simply become its own kind of unproductive anxiety rather than a genuine safeguard. The research this chapter draws on doesn't argue for infinite, unbounded scrutiny of every decision forever — that would trade one problem for another, and a companion volume in this library addresses the cost of compulsive, anxiety-driven over-checking directly. The specific claim here is narrower: checking behaviors that were deliberately built into an earlier, more diligent period of a person's or a group's financial life deserve an active, ongoing decision about whether to keep them, rather than a passive, unexamined erosion driven by nothing more than accumulating confidence. The goal isn't maximal checking. It's checking that survives an honest, periodic reassessment of whether it's still needed, rather than checking that simply fades because nobody consciously decided it should stop.

What it costs you

The most direct cost is the one both scenes illustrate: checking behaviors — comparing against a benchmark, seeking a second opinion, reviewing disclosures and documentation carefully — are not simply beginner's training wheels that a genuinely skilled person outgrows. They're an ongoing, permanent mechanism for catching the specific gap between actual skill and self-assessed skill that this entire book has been documenting, and abandoning them doesn't reflect having outgrown the need for them. It reflects having lost the specific practice that was helping keep the gap from widening unchecked.

There's a second cost that compounds specifically because the gap between actual performance and self-assessed performance, once it starts widening due to reduced checking, tends to widen at an accelerating rate rather than a steady one — each unchecked period increases confidence somewhat, per the mechanisms in earlier chapters, and increased confidence further reduces the perceived need for checking, creating a feedback loop directly analogous to the escalation dynamic described in Chapter 6, but applied to self-monitoring rather than to position sizing.

A third cost shows up specifically for people whose financial decisions affect others — the advisor whose clients are relying on the checking behaviors she's quietly stopped, the fund manager whose investors assume a level of ongoing diligence that experience has, in reality, gradually eroded. The cost of reduced self-checking in these cases isn't confined to the person experiencing the overconfidence. It's distributed across everyone whose financial well-being depends on that person's ongoing, active diligence rather than on a reputation built from an earlier period when the diligence was still fully intact.

A fourth cost, illustrated by the drifting partnership, is specific to groups rather than individuals: once a rigorous process erodes informally, rebuilding it requires someone to openly name that the group's trust in itself has outpaced its actual current practice — a genuinely uncomfortable conversation to initiate precisely because it requires questioning colleagues' judgment during a period the group's own results suggest that judgment has never been better. The better the recent results, the harder this specific conversation becomes to start, which means the erosion this chapter describes tends to go furthest, and become hardest to reverse, in exactly the groups whose success would seem, from the outside, to argue against any need for concern at all.

A fifth cost, illustrated by the household whose subscription error went unnoticed for years, is the specific way small, individually minor lapses accumulate silently once a review habit lapses. No single missed month of that subscription fee would have mattered on its own. What mattered was the multi-year absence of the review process that would have caught it in month one instead of year three — the cost isn't really the subscription fee itself, small as it was. It's everything else, of unknown size, that the same lapsed habit may also be quietly failing to catch, invisible precisely because nobody is looking closely enough anymore to know what else might be there.

How this shows up without you noticing

Notice the specific word "formality" attached to a practice you used to take seriously. "I don't really need to run the full checklist anymore" or "that step feels like a formality at this point" are both worth pausing on, because they describe the exact moment a genuine safeguard quietly gets reclassified as unnecessary friction. The practice rarely gets abandoned all at once, with a deliberate decision behind it. It gets abandoned one skipped instance at a time, each one small enough to feel harmless, until the accumulated skipping becomes the new, unexamined normal.

The overrides

Treat checking behaviors as permanent infrastructure, not a beginner's phase to graduate out of. Whatever specific practices — a benchmark comparison, a documented decision log, a second opinion sought on sizable decisions — served you well early on, keep them in place explicitly as ongoing structure, not because you doubt your growing skill, but because the specific research on this pattern suggests skill and self-monitoring are separate capacities, and only one of them automatically improves with experience.

Actively seek out disagreement, on a set schedule, rather than waiting for it to arrive uninvited. Because feedback-seeking naturally declines as perceived expertise grows, counteract the decline deliberately: build a standing practice of asking someone specifically for the strongest case against your current approach, on a regular schedule, rather than relying on disagreement to find you on its own — because at higher levels of perceived expertise, it increasingly won't.

Distinguish explicitly between skill at the activity and skill at evaluating your own performance in it. Periodically ask yourself directly whether your self-assessment practices have kept pace with your growing experience, or whether they've quietly atrophied while your confidence continued climbing independent of them. These are separate questions, and only an honest answer to the second one protects you from the gap this chapter describes.

Notice when asking for feedback starts to feel like an admission of weakness, and treat that feeling as information rather than as a reason to stop asking. If seeking critique on a decision now carries a social cost it didn't carry earlier in your career or investing history, that changed cost is worth naming explicitly — and worth pushing past deliberately, since the social discomfort of asking is a poor guide to how useful the answer would actually be.

Audit your own recent decisions against your own earlier standards, honestly, at least annually. Pull out whatever checklist, process, or standard you used to hold yourself to in an earlier, more explicitly diligent period, and apply it to your current decisions exactly as written. If your current practice wouldn't pass the standard your earlier, more careful self would have applied, that gap is worth taking seriously rather than dismissing as an outdated formality you've since outgrown.

If you lead or work within a group, build structured dissent into the process formally, not informally. Assign a rotating devil's-advocate role for major decisions, or require a documented case against any proposal before it's approved, rather than relying on whoever happens to feel comfortable enough to disagree out loud that day. A structural requirement survives a team's growing confidence in itself; an informal norm of openness usually doesn't.

Ask a newer, less experienced colleague or partner what they'd want to know before trusting your judgment. Someone earlier in their own experience is often better positioned to notice which of your checking habits have quietly disappeared, precisely because they don't yet share your settled assumptions about which steps are "obviously" no longer necessary. Their outside, less acclimated view is a genuine asset — treat it as one rather than as a lack of experience to be politely tolerated.

Reassess your checking habits on a fixed schedule, not only when something goes wrong. Waiting for a mistake to reveal that a safeguard has quietly eroded means the safeguard has already failed once before you notice. Set a specific, calendared review of your own checking practices — quarterly or annually — rather than relying on a bad outcome to be the thing that finally prompts the reassessment.

Name the specific checking behaviors you had in your first year, and compare them line by line against what you actually do now. Vague impressions of "I used to be more careful" are easy to dismiss. A specific, itemized comparison — this exact checklist, this exact review cadence, this exact second-opinion habit — makes the erosion considerably harder to wave away as simply the natural, harmless evolution of growing expertise.

If you're near the height of your own career or track record, treat that specifically as a prompt to reinstate structure, not relax it. The veteran portfolio manager's junior analysts stopped challenging her decisions precisely during her most distinguished years, exactly the period a reasonable observer might assume required the least additional scrutiny. Recognize that assumption as backwards: the years when your judgment carries the most unquestioned weight are the years an outside challenge is hardest to get and therefore most valuable to deliberately preserve.

Confidence that stops checking itself isn't evidence of expertise — it's evidence that the one mechanism capable of catching the gap between what you actually know and what you believe you know has been quietly switched off, usually at exactly the moment the gap has the most room to grow.

Chapter 9 — The Founder Who Bet the Company Twice

What Happens When the Overconfidence Instinct Gets Applied at the Largest Possible Scale

The first company he built succeeded against odds that, examined honestly afterward, were genuinely long — a crowded market, thin initial funding, a launch timed by circumstances well outside his control that happened to land favorably. He tells the story of that success as a story about vision, persistence, and a willingness to bet aggressively when more cautious advisors around him counseled a smaller, safer approach — a story with some genuine truth in it, since real skill and real persistence were part of what happened, alongside the considerable good fortune of timing and market conditions he had no hand in creating. By the time he starts the second company, several years later, the story has fully hardened into a personal doctrine: bold, aggressive bets, sized well beyond what conventional caution would recommend, are simply how meaningful success actually gets built, and the earlier caution he'd overridden the first time is treated, retrospectively, as an obstacle he was right to ignore rather than as a reasonable, risk-appropriate concern that happened not to materialize.

The second company is funded, from its earliest stage, at a scale and a pace that dwarfs how the first one actually started — larger initial spending, faster hiring, a bet-the-company approach to a single, unproven strategic direction rather than the more incremental, option-preserving approach that, examined honestly, the first company had actually followed in its own earliest and most fragile months, whatever the founder's retold story about it now claims. The market conditions this time are considerably less favorable, a fact that was reasonably knowable in advance and was, in fact, raised by more than one advisor during the second company's early planning — concerns the founder waves off with the same confident dismissal that, in his own retelling of the first company's story, had been vindicated once already. The second company fails, expensively, within two years, having consumed both the founder's personal wealth from the first company's success and a considerable amount of investor capital raised largely on the strength of his first company's track record — a track record that, on the closer, more honest examination this book has spent its chapters encouraging, always contained more luck than the confident, retold version of the story ever fully acknowledged.

A second scene, considerably smaller in scale but built from the identical mechanism, plays out inside a household rather than a boardroom. A couple who paid off a modest inheritance-funded down payment on a rental property and sold it two years later for a genuinely strong profit — driven substantially by a broad, regional run-up in property values that lifted virtually every comparable owner in the area — describes the sale, in conversation with friends considering their own first investment property, as proof of a specific, replicable formula they've now mastered: buy underpriced, renovate lightly, hold briefly, sell into strength. On the strength of that formula, they use the proceeds, along with a considerably larger loan than the first property required, to buy two additional properties simultaneously in a different, unfamiliar market they've never actually invested in before, reasoning that the formula that worked once will simply repeat. Both purchases are made within the same eight-week window, without the kind of neighborhood-specific research the first, successful purchase happened to receive almost by accident, because the couple, at the time of the first deal, hadn't yet decided they had a formula worth trusting blindly.

A third scene shows the pattern at an intermediate scale, inside a professional career rather than a company or a household. A consultant whose first independent client engagement, taken on a whim after leaving a stable salaried position, turns into an unusually large and lucrative contract almost immediately, describes the transition afterward as proof that she'd been "underselling herself for years" in traditional employment — a conclusion that treats one unusually fortunate first client, who happened to have an urgent, high-budget need at exactly the moment she became available, as evidence of a durable, general market value rather than a single favorable match of timing and circumstance. She raises her rates considerably for her second and third clients, sized to the confidence the first contract produced rather than to any broader evidence about what the market would actually bear, and loses both prospective engagements to competitors pricing more conventionally, a result she initially attributes to those particular prospects simply not recognizing her value, rather than to a rate genuinely calibrated by a single data point.

A fourth scene closes this chapter's opening at the smallest scale it covers, worth including because it shows the identical mechanism operating with almost no money at stake at all. A hobbyist who sells a handmade item at a local craft fair for considerably more than expected, purely because a well-known local collector happened to be browsing that specific table that specific afternoon, decides on the strength of that single sale to quit a stable part-time job and commit to selling full-time at a self-funded booth in a much larger regional market the following month — a decision made without any further research into whether the same price point, or anything close to it, would hold up with a broader, less specifically motivated audience. The regional market, when it arrives, produces a small fraction of the first sale's price for comparable items, a result the hobbyist initially attributes to the new market simply "not appreciating quality work" rather than to the original sale having been an unusually favorable, largely unrepeatable match between one specific buyer and one specific item.

What's actually happening

This chapter's scene draws together every mechanism named across the preceding eight chapters and shows them operating simultaneously, at a scale where the stakes are no longer a single trading account but an entire enterprise and the livelihoods connected to it. Research on this specific pattern exists at the corporate and executive level, and it applies directly here, because it demonstrates that the pattern this book has been tracking in individual investors and gamblers scales up, largely unchanged, to some of the highest-stakes financial decision-makers in the economy.

Economists Colin Camerer and Dan Lovallo, in influential research on what they termed excess entry into competitive markets, found that entrepreneurs and business decision-makers systematically overestimate their own relative chances of success when entering a competitive venture, a pattern their experiments traced directly to the overplacement mechanism discussed in Chapter 4 — a strong, general tendency for people to rate their own skill as above average, applied specifically to the decision of whether and how aggressively to enter a new competitive venture. Camerer and Lovallo's research found that this overplacement was considerably stronger specifically among people who had prior experience with some earlier success, exactly the pattern illustrated by this chapter's founder: an initial success appears not to produce a more calibrated, honestly weighted assessment of the odds on a second venture, but a less calibrated one, precisely because the first success gets processed through the self-serving attribution mechanism from Chapter 1 and converted into an inflated, durable belief in personal entrepreneurial skill.

There's directly relevant research at an even larger corporate scale, conducted by economists Ulrike Malmendier and Geoffrey Tate, examining the investment and acquisition behavior of corporate chief executives whose personal characteristics suggested elevated overconfidence — measured, in their research, through indicators including executives' own patterns of holding company stock options longer than a purely rational risk-management strategy would predict, itself a signal of excessive confidence in their own company's continued success. Malmendier and Tate found that CEOs identified as more overconfident by these measures made systematically different, and on average worse, corporate investment and acquisition decisions than their less overconfident peers — overpaying for acquisitions more frequently, over-investing when internal cash was available regardless of the actual quality of the investment opportunity, and showing a measurably reduced sensitivity to external, more objective signals that might have contradicted their own optimistic internal assessment. Their research provides some of the clearest, most consequential evidence available that this book's subject isn't confined to individual retail investors or recreational gamblers — it operates at the scale of major corporate capital allocation decisions, made by people whose formal qualifications and demonstrated prior competence would, on paper, suggest they should be considerably less susceptible to it than an amateur trader, and yet the research finds they are not.

A further, specific mechanism, unique to this largest-scale version of the pattern, combines several earlier chapters' findings: escalation of commitment, a well-documented organizational behavior finding, distinct from but closely related to this book's broader subject, describing the tendency for decision-makers to continue investing in a failing course of action specifically because of the resources already committed to it — a pattern first studied in depth by researcher Barry Staw. What makes the founder's second-company story a particularly potent combination is that escalation of commitment and the overconfidence instinct this book describes reinforce each other directly: the founder's inflated confidence, built from the first company's success, drove an oversized initial bet on the second company; and once early warning signs emerged that the second bet was struggling, the sunk investment already committed created additional pressure to continue rather than reassess, a pressure that a person already primed by overconfidence to dismiss external warning signs is especially poorly positioned to resist.

The household scale of this pattern deserves its own attention, too, rather than being treated as simply a smaller version of the corporate story. Camerer and Lovallo's excess-entry research and Malmendier and Tate's executive research were both conducted on populations with at least some institutional guardrails around them — boards, investors, disclosure requirements, external oversight of some kind, however imperfect. A household making a second, larger real-estate bet on the strength of one successful first flip typically has none of these guardrails at all. There's no board to raise the concern the more cautious partner might privately feel but not fully voice, no outside investor whose due diligence might catch a gap in the couple's unfamiliarity with the new market. The mechanism is identical to the corporate version. The correction mechanisms available to catch it before it becomes expensive are considerably weaker, which makes this smaller-scale version of the pattern, if anything, more dangerous relative to the resources involved, not less.

This chapter's research discussion should close with an honest note on what Malmendier and Tate's work does and doesn't establish, since this book has tried throughout to represent its citations precisely. Their research identifies a correlation between measured executive overconfidence and worse average investment and acquisition outcomes — it does not claim that every confident executive makes bad decisions, or that caution alone reliably produces better ones. Some of the boldest, most aggressive corporate bets in economic history have paid off spectacularly, and no honest reading of this research pretends otherwise. What the research supports is narrower and, for this book's purposes, sufficient: on average, across a large number of decision-makers and decisions, the specific psychological signature of overconfidence measured independently of any single outcome predicts worse subsequent decisions, a population-level finding entirely consistent with any individual overconfident decision-maker still getting lucky, sometimes repeatedly, before the underlying pattern eventually catches up with them.

What it costs you

At this scale, the costs described throughout this book compound into something categorically larger than a single bad trade or an overleveraged personal portfolio. The direct financial cost is the most visible: personal wealth, investor capital, and often the livelihoods of employees hired on the strength of an initial, aggressive bet, all exposed to a risk sized not by an honest assessment of the second venture's actual odds, but by a confidence level built substantially from the retold, oversimplified story of a first success that always contained more luck than the story acknowledged.

There's a second, less visible cost specific to this scale: because the founder's overconfidence was validated once, by an actual, real success, the specific correction mechanisms available to a less experienced or less successful decision-maker — outside skepticism, a board or investor group's caution, an advisor's warning — become considerably less effective, precisely because the founder now has a genuine, real track record to point to as evidence that betting boldly against conventional caution is exactly the right approach. Success, at this scale, doesn't just inflate the founder's own confidence. It inflates other people's willingness to defer to that confidence, which removes exactly the kind of outside correction that might otherwise have caught the second venture's risk before it became unrecoverable.

A third cost is what happens after the failure, and it connects directly back to Chapter 7's mechanism operating at full institutional scale: the story told afterward about why the second venture failed rarely lands squarely on the decision to bet as aggressively as the founder did, in circumstances considerably less favorable than the first company's, against specific warnings raised in advance. It lands, far more often, on external market conditions, on timing, on factors the story frames as unforeseeable — precisely the same self-protective narrative rewrite this book has documented at every smaller scale, now applied to a failure large enough to have cost investors, employees, and the founder's own family a genuinely consequential amount, with a story still built to protect the same confidence that produced the loss in the first place.

A fourth cost, visible clearly in the household scene, is what happens to a family's total financial resilience when a single successful bet gets treated as a repeatable formula rather than an unusually favorable, largely unrepeated set of conditions. Concentrating a considerably larger share of household wealth into two simultaneous, under-researched purchases, in an unfamiliar market, leaves a family with far less capacity to absorb a downturn than the original, single, well-timed property ever put at risk — a structural increase in fragility that arrived disguised, the entire time, as evidence of increasing financial sophistication.

A fifth cost, illustrated by the consultant's mispriced second and third engagements, is the specific way this pattern can quietly narrow a person's future opportunities rather than simply costing money directly. Pricing herself against a single, unrepeatable data point cost her two engagements she might otherwise have won at a more conventionally calibrated rate — a cost that never shows up as a loss on any account statement, because it's an opportunity that simply never happened, invisible in exactly the way this book's earlier chapters have described the road-not-taken cost of an inflated sense of one's own established value.

How this shows up without you noticing

Listen for the word "formula," or its close cousins "playbook" and "blueprint," applied to a single successful outcome. A real, tested formula requires repetition across genuinely varied conditions before it's earned that name. A single success, however satisfying, is a story — and the word a person reaches for to describe it, "formula" versus "one thing that happened to work," is itself a useful early signal of how much weight that single data point is quietly being asked to carry.

The overrides

Treat a first major success as a single, small data point, not as a proven formula, regardless of how large the success actually was. One success, however large, is still one data point about the actual ratio of skill to luck involved — genuinely insufficient, on its own, to establish a durable, repeatable formula, no matter how compelling the retold story of that first success eventually becomes.

Build outside challenge into any decision structurally, before the stakes get large enough for confidence to override it. At the scale this chapter describes, informal willingness to hear disagreement isn't sufficient protection — build a formal requirement for genuine, empowered outside challenge into any major decision, structured so that dismissing the challenge requires more than simply overriding it in the room, the same way a board, an independent advisor, or a formal pre-mortem process is designed to function.

Separate the decision to continue investing from the amount already invested. When early warning signs emerge on a large commitment, deliberately evaluate the decision to continue as though starting fresh, ignoring the resources already sunk into the venture — a practiced discipline directly targeting the escalation-of-commitment dynamic, which by design makes prior investment feel like a reason to continue rather than the irrelevant, already-spent cost it actually is for the purposes of evaluating what to do next.

Ask what a genuinely skeptical outsider, with no stake in your prior success, would say about the current bet. Specifically imagine, or better, actually consult, someone with real domain expertise and no personal or financial investment in validating your prior track record. Their honest assessment, unclouded by any stake in your continued success, is often the clearest available signal of whether the current decision is genuinely well-supported or substantially a product of confidence the first success never actually earned.

Size the second bet to the actual, honestly assessed odds of the second venture — not to the emotional weight of the first one's success. The conditions, market, timing, and specific risks of a second major venture are rarely identical to the first, however similar the story feels in the retelling. Evaluate the second bet on its own actual merits and its own actual odds, independent of how much confidence the first success generated.

Write down, before the second bet, exactly how much of the first success you honestly attribute to conditions outside your control. Force yourself to put a specific, honest estimate on paper — not zero, and not everything — before sizing anything against the strength of that first success. A written estimate is far harder to quietly inflate after the fact than an unexamined, comfortable sense that the first win was "mostly me."

Build in a mandatory waiting period between a major success and any decision to bet a comparable or larger amount again. The pull to move quickly, to capitalize on momentum, on a reputation, on investor enthusiasm still warm from the first success, is exactly the pressure most likely to short-circuit honest evaluation. A fixed, pre-committed waiting period — long enough for the initial excitement to settle — protects the second decision from being made inside the emotional afterglow of the first.

If you're advising, funding, or partnering with someone riding a recent major success, apply extra scrutiny rather than extra deference. The instinct to defer more readily to someone whose judgment was recently, visibly validated runs directly counter to what this chapter's research actually recommends. A recent win is exactly the moment a decision-maker's judgment most needs an outside check, not the moment that check becomes least welcome or most readily waived.

If you've had a genuinely large recent success, tell the story of it to someone with permission to interrupt and ask hard questions. Choose a specific person — a partner, a trusted colleague, a mentor with no stake in flattering you — and narrate the success in detail, explicitly inviting them to interrupt with skeptical questions as you go, rather than saving questions for the end. The interruptions themselves, not just the eventual feedback, are what keep a retold success story honest rather than smoothing itself into an increasingly confident, increasingly unexamined legend.

Before committing significant new resources on the strength of a single strong result, ask whether the result would need to repeat, or merely be explained, to justify the next bet. A genuine formula should survive being tested a second time under different conditions before it's trusted with meaningfully more resources. A single result only needs an explanation, not a repetition, and mistaking the second for the first is precisely how one favorable outcome ends up financing a considerably larger bet than the evidence has actually earned.

A single win, however large, is still a sample size of one. Betting the whole enterprise a second time on the strength of a first success that was never fully examined for how much of it was luck is the most expensive possible version of every mistake this book has named — and it is, without fail, available to anyone who's ever won big enough, once, to stop asking why.

Before You Go

There's a version of this book that could have argued the opposite of everything it's actually said — that confidence itself is the enemy, that every win should be treated with suspicion, that the safest financial life is the one lived in permanent, careful doubt about your own judgment. That would have been a simpler argument to make, and it would have been wrong, in a way worth explicitly disowning before you close these pages. Confidence isn't the problem this book has been describing. Miscalibrated confidence is — confidence that's grown larger than the actual evidence for it, quietly, one flattering interpretation of an ambiguous outcome at a time, until the size of your next bet reflects a track record that was never actually as strong as it felt.

Real skill exists, in investing and in every other domain this book has touched. Some people really do develop a genuine, durable edge through years of deliberate practice, honest feedback, and disciplined evaluation of their own results — and nothing in these nine chapters is meant to talk a genuinely skilled person out of trusting real, well-earned confidence. The entire task this book has set out to do is narrower than that, and more useful: giving you a way to tell the difference between the confidence a result actually earns and the confidence a result merely feels like it earns, because those two things, from the inside, in the moment a win lands, feel identical — and only one of them should be setting the size of what you risk next.

Plainly, too: the goal of everything in this book was never to make you a smaller, more timid version of yourself. A reader who finishes these nine chapters and concludes the safest response is to stop taking any risk at all has missed the point as thoroughly as a reader who takes nothing away and keeps betting exactly as before. The actual goal, threaded through every chapter, is calibration — sizing your confidence, and the bets built on top of it, to match the evidence that genuinely supports them, no more and no less. Sometimes that means betting smaller than the story in your head wants you to. Sometimes, for a genuinely skilled decision honestly under-trusted out of excess caution, it means betting more. The overrides in this book aren't a one-directional brake. They're a way of checking the story against the evidence, in either direction, before the story gets to decide the size on its own.

Look back, briefly, across the range of scenes this book has walked through. The trader whose ledger only really counted the wins as evidence about himself. The investor whose hand-picked positions felt safer for reasons that had nothing to do with actual odds. The bettor whose streak felt like momentum when the math said it was noise. The nearly universal, quietly impossible belief that each of us is better than most other people at whatever we happen to be doing. The near-miss that lied about how close it actually came. The position that grew larger with every win until the loss that finally arrived was bigger than everything that came before it combined. The story that rewrote a loss until it pointed at anyone except the decision that actually produced it. The expert who stopped checking exactly when checking mattered most. And the founder who bet the whole enterprise a second time on a first success that was never as fully earned as its retelling claimed. Nine different scenes, nine different scales of money, one identical mechanism running underneath every single one of them.

One final honest note about what this book cannot do for you. It cannot make winning feel any less like proof of your own skill — that feeling is close to a permanent, structural feature of how a mind processes a favorable outcome, not a bug this book has any hope of patching out through nine chapters of explanation. The next time a genuinely ambiguous bet pays off, you will very likely still feel, at least for a moment, the same settled, comfortable certainty this book has spent its length describing: *you saw something. You were right.* What can change, if these chapters have done their job, isn't that first feeling. It's what happens in the specific, narrow window right after it — whether you let the feeling walk straight through to the size of your next bet unexamined, the way it likely has every time before now, or whether some small, trained part of you pauses long enough to ask the one question that actually matters: how much of this was really me, and how much of it was simply the world going my way this time.

That question is the whole practice, and it is worth saying plainly that it never gets easier to ask sincerely, no matter how many times you've asked it before. Every win will keep arriving with its own ready-made, flattering story attached, because that's what a mind built the way yours is built does with a favorable, ambiguous outcome — it always will, at every scale, for the rest of your financial life, whether the bet in question is a hundred dollars or the entire company you've built. The overrides in this book don't promise to make that story stop arriving. They only promise to widen the gap between the story arriving and you acting on it, long enough for one honest, harder question to get a word in before the next bet gets sized.

It helps, too, to say what success actually looks like if this book has done its job, because it will not look dramatic. It will not look like a moment of sudden, permanent clarity, and it will not look like the disappearance of the feeling this whole book has been describing. It will look considerably smaller and quieter than that: a specific afternoon, months or years from now, when a bet pays off in a way that feels like proof, and you pause — not for long, just long enough — and open the written record instead of trusting the story. You compare what you actually reasoned at the time against what actually happened, and either the record supports the flattering conclusion or it doesn't, and either way, you now know something true instead of something merely felt. That's the whole outcome this book has been built to produce. Not a different feeling. A different habit, sitting quietly next to the feeling, ready exactly when the feeling arrives.

If you take away only one practical habit from everything in this book, let it be the written record described across nearly every chapter's overrides — reasoning and confidence, written down, before the outcome is known. Every other override in this book is a variation on that same single idea, applied to a different specific moment in the pattern. If you build only one piece of structure, build that one first. It is, more than any other single habit this book describes, the actual mechanism by which a flattering story gets checked against what was really known, and really believed, before the outcome arrived to rewrite it.

Remember, too, that every scene in this book — the trader, the poker player, the entrepreneur, the founder, the couple co-signing a loan — started out as someone who simply took a chance and had it work. None of them set out to become a cautionary example. They arrived there through a sequence of individually reasonable-feeling steps, each one following naturally from the step before it, with no single moment along the way that felt like a decision to abandon caution. That's the genuinely uncomfortable truth underneath this entire book: the pattern doesn't announce itself as recklessness while it's happening. It announces itself as growing competence, growing confidence, growing proof that the bet you took a chance on paid off because you were right to take it. The only real defense against a pattern that disguises itself this well is a habit that doesn't depend on recognizing the disguise in the moment — which is exactly what the written record, and every override built on top of it, is for.

One last thought before these pages are yours. Somewhere ahead of you, likely sooner than you expect, something is going to go right — a trade, a pitch, a bet, a decision made on instinct that happens to land exactly where you hoped it would. In that moment, you won't need to remember every researcher's name or every chapter's specific scene. You'll only need to remember one sentence, the one this whole book has been building toward since its first page: *winning doesn't mean I was right. It means, this time, I wasn't wrong — and those are not the same thing, no matter how identical they feel the instant the result comes in.* Say that sentence, mean it, and let it buy you the handful of seconds this entire book was written to protect. That's not a large thing to ask of yourself. It is, in the end, nearly the whole difference between a track record you can actually trust and one you've simply never looked at closely enough to doubt.

Notes & Further Reading

The psychological and behavioral-finance concepts referenced throughout this book draw on established, verifiable research. Readers interested in going deeper are pointed toward the original sources and researchers credited in each chapter, rather than toward secondary summaries. A general note on how this list is organized: entries are grouped by the chapter in which the concept first appears, though several concepts — self-serving attribution, hindsight bias, and mental accounting among them — recur across multiple chapters, since the whole argument of this book rests on showing that a small number of underlying mechanisms produce a much wider range of surface-level financial behavior.

On self-serving attribution bias: Dale Miller and Michael Ross's review of the experimental literature on self-serving biases in attribution, published in the mid-1970s, established the foundational finding underlying Chapter 1 — that people systematically attribute successes to internal, stable factors and failures to external, unstable ones. Related foundational work on causal attribution more broadly, developed by Fritz Heider and later formalized by Bernard Weiner into a fuller theory of achievement-related attribution, underlies the internal/external and stable/unstable framework discussed in that chapter.

On hindsight bias: Baruch Fischhoff's research on the "knew it all along" effect, demonstrating that people consistently overestimate how predictable a known outcome was beforehand, informs the discussion in both Chapter 1 and Chapter 7.

On the illusion of control: Ellen Langer's foundational 1975 research, including her widely cited lottery-ticket experiments, established the illusion-of-control effect discussed in Chapter 2, along with her identification of the specific factors — choice, familiarity, competition, and active involvement — that reliably strengthen it.

On the hot-hand fallacy and its later reconsideration: Thomas Gilovich, Robert Vallone, and Amos Tversky's 1985 study of basketball shooting data and player and fan beliefs established the original hot-hand fallacy finding discussed in Chapter 3. The later reanalysis by economists Joshua Miller and

Adam Sanjurjo, identifying a statistical bias in how the original research measured streaks and finding evidence for small genuine hot-hand effects once corrected for, is presented in that chapter as an honest and important complication of the original, more widely popularized finding.

On the law of small numbers: Daniel Kahneman and Amos Tversky's earlier research on the tendency to expect small samples of random data to resemble the properties of a larger population more closely than they actually do underlies the broader discussion of streak perception in Chapter 3.

On illusory superiority and overconfidence taxonomy: Ola Svenson's 1981 study of self-rated driving skill established the foundational better-than-average finding discussed in Chapter 4. The distinction between overestimation, overplacement, and overprecision as separate forms of overconfidence, developed by researchers Don Moore and Paul Healy, provides the more precise framework used throughout that chapter and referenced again in Chapter 9.

On gender and trading behavior: Research by economists Brad Barber and Terrance Odean, examining large datasets of brokerage account activity, documented differences in average trading frequency and net returns associated with measured overconfidence differences, referenced in Chapter 4 and discussed more extensively in Chapter 6, including their research published under the title "Trading Is Hazardous to Your Wealth."

On the near-miss effect: Robert Reid's foundational 1986 research on how near-misses are processed differently from clear losses in gambling behavior, and neuroscientist Luke Clark's subsequent brain-imaging research on the reward-related neural response to near-misses, underlie the discussion in Chapter 5.

On counterfactual thinking: Research on how people generate and emotionally weight mental simulations of alternative outcomes, including well-known findings on Olympic medalists' satisfaction levels, informs the discussion of near-miss framing in Chapter 5.

On escalating risk-taking following gains: Brad Barber and Terrance Odean's broader body of research on individual investor trading behavior underlies the discussion in Chapter 6 of how gains drive subsequent increases in trading frequency and position size.

On outcome bias: Jonathan Baron and John Hershey's foundational 1988 paper on outcome bias, demonstrating that people evaluate the quality of a past decision based on how it turned out rather than on the reasonableness of the decision given information available at the time, underlies the central argument of Chapter 7.

On cognitive dissonance: Leon Festinger's foundational theory of cognitive dissonance, describing the psychological discomfort produced by holding contradictory beliefs and the motivated resolution of that discomfort, informs the discussion in Chapter 7 of how a loss's story gets rewritten to protect a person's broader self-image.

On the Dunning-Kruger effect and its limits: Justin Kruger and David Dunning's 1999 research on the relationship between low competence and inflated self-assessment established the foundational finding discussed in Chapter 8. This book presents the finding with the specific caveats later research and reanalysis have raised about the popularized, oversimplified version of the effect, rather than the broader, less well-supported claims sometimes attributed to it.

On positive illusions: Shelley Taylor and Jonathon Brown's influential research on mildly inflated self-perceptions as a psychologically normal and often functionally useful feature of well-adjusted people informs the more nuanced discussion in Chapter 8 of when positive illusion serves a person well and when it becomes costly.

On excess entry and entrepreneurial overconfidence: Economists Colin Camerer and Dan Lovallo's research on excess entry into competitive markets, tracing entrepreneurial overplacement to prior experience with success, underlies the discussion in Chapter 9.

On executive overconfidence and corporate investment: Economists Ulrike Malmendier and Geoffrey Tate's research examining the relationship between measured CEO overconfidence and corporate investment and acquisition decisions provides the corporate-scale evidence discussed in Chapter 9.

On escalation of commitment: Researcher Barry Staw's foundational work on escalation of commitment to a failing course of action, driven by prior resource investment, informs the discussion in Chapter 9 of how overconfidence and sunk-cost dynamics reinforce each other at the largest scale this book covers.

Additional concepts referenced across chapters. Confirmation bias, referenced in Chapter 1, describes the well-documented general tendency to favor information consistent with an existing belief over information that challenges it, a foundational concept in cognitive psychology studied across decades of research into reasoning and belief maintenance. The illusion of validity, referenced in Chapter 2, is discussed in Daniel Kahneman's broader writing on judgment and decision-making, describing how subjective confidence often tracks the internal coherence of a story rather than the statistical quality of the evidence behind it. The omission-commission distinction in regret, referenced in Chapter 7, describing the finding that people experience more intense regret over losses resulting from an active decision than from an equivalent loss resulting from inaction, has been studied across behavioral decision research examining how the structure of a decision shapes the emotional weight assigned to its outcome. Research on structured dissent and group decision-making, referenced in Chapter 8, examining how formal mechanisms for eliciting disagreement improve decision quality specifically in groups with a strong prior track record, draws on the broader organizational-behavior literature on groupthink and decision quality that also informs a companion volume in this library's discussion of cascading group fear.

A note on the honest limits of the hot-hand research specifically, since Chapter 3 treats it with unusual care: the finding has undergone a genuine, substantive scientific reconsideration since its original 1985 publication, and this book has tried throughout to represent that reconsideration accurately rather than repeating either the original, more sweeping claim or the popularized version of it uncritically. Readers interested in the technical details of the Miller and Sanjurjo reanalysis, involving a subtle selection bias in how conditional streak probabilities were originally calculated, are encouraged to consult their published work directly rather than secondary summaries, which have not always represented the correction accurately.

On dopamine and variable reward. The broader neuroscience of reward prediction and variable reinforcement, referenced in Chapter 6, draws on decades of research into how the brain's dopamine systems respond to unpredictable versus predictable rewards, a body of work spanning both animal and human studies that underlies much of the modern understanding of motivation, reward-seeking, and the psychology of gambling more broadly.

On the design of near-miss mechanics in gambling products. Research into the deliberate engineering of near-miss rates in electronic gaming machines, referenced in Chapter 5, has been documented across studies of gambling-industry design practices and regulatory research into responsible-gambling safeguards, an area of applied research distinct from but closely related to Reid's and Clark's foundational academic work on the underlying psychological effect.

A final honest note on this book's overall approach to citation: readers will notice that most named research in these pages describes general tendencies documented across populations, not guarantees about any specific individual's behavior. Every person is different, and every reader will recognize themselves in some of these chapters more than others. That variation is expected and doesn't undermine the underlying research — it reflects the ordinary, honest limits of what psychological science can tell you about any one person's specific financial life, as opposed to what it can tell you, reliably, about the general shape of how a human mind under these conditions tends to behave.

A note on replication and the current state of behavioral-finance research more broadly: several of the specific findings cited across this book, including the original hot-hand research discussed at length in Chapter 3, have undergone genuine scientific reconsideration since their original publication, a normal and healthy part of how psychological science progresses over time. Where a finding's status has meaningfully evolved since its original publication, this book has tried to say so explicitly rather than presenting a decades-old result as though it were still the field's final word. Readers should expect the same of any future edition of this book, and of the broader field this book draws from — behavioral science is an active, ongoing area of research, not a closed, settled body of permanent fact.

This book does not cite any statistic, study, or survey not directly attributable to a named researcher or well-established body of research. Where a mechanism is described without a specific citation, it reflects general, widely accepted psychological principles rather than a single study, and readers are encouraged to consult the primary sources above for the full depth of the underlying research.

This book is not financial advice. It does not recommend any specific investment, account, platform, or allocation strategy, and nothing in it should be treated as a substitute for guidance from a qualified financial professional familiar with your specific circumstances. Its subject is behavioral: the psychology of overconfidence following a favorable outcome, not the question of what you should actually hold, sell, or buy. Scenarios and individuals described throughout the chapters are illustrative composites, not case studies of specific real people, and are not attributed to any named research.

About

The Overconfidence Instinct is part of a library exploring the wired-in patterns that shape how people relate to money — not as a series of character flaws to overcome through willpower, but as a set of honest, researched mechanisms built into every human nervous system, worth understanding on their own terms. Each book in the library isolates one distinct pattern, traces it to its real psychological roots, and offers concrete, decision-level ways to work with it rather than against it.

This is not a book of investment advice, product recommendations, or step-by-step financial planning. It doesn't tell you which account to open, which position to take, or what percentage of anything to risk. What it offers instead is narrower and, hopefully, more durable: a clear enough understanding of one specific mental pattern that you can recognize it the next time it's operating on you, in whatever form your next win happens to take.

If this book was useful, the rest of the library covers other patterns worth knowing — the way earned income quietly expands to fill whatever room a raise creates, the way secrecy around money compounds quietly inside a relationship, the way acute fear can override a lifetime of careful financial planning in the space of a few seconds, the way sudden money gets spent faster than earned money simply because of how it arrived, and the way an invisible ceiling keeps otherwise capable people from ever asking for what they're worth. Each book takes the same approach this one did: a real, named psychological mechanism, shown through close, recognizable scenes rather than abstractions, paired with overrides that live in your own judgment rather than in any specific product or platform.

Every book in this library is built the same way: one pattern, traced honestly to real research, translated into overrides you can actually use under pressure rather than only in hindsight. None of them promise to remove the pattern they describe. All of them are trying to do the one thing that actually holds up under real conditions — widen the gap between the moment the pattern fires and the moment you act on it, until there's room in that gap for a calmer, more complete version of your own judgment to have a say.

None of these books ask you to become a different kind of person. They ask you to notice, honestly and without judgment, which specific pattern tends to run the show when a result — good or bad — lands in front of you, and then to build one small, concrete piece of structure around that specific pattern, in advance, while you're calm enough to build it well. That's the entire method, repeated across every pattern this library covers. It isn't dramatic. It doesn't promise transformation. It just quietly works, one widened gap at a time, which turns out to be exactly the kind of unglamorous, durable progress that actually holds up on the days a win is trying hardest to convince you of something your own honest track record hasn't actually earned.

The library's premise is a simple one, worth stating plainly here since it underlies every volume: most financial advice targets the wrong layer of the problem. It assumes the gap between what people know and what people actually do is a knowledge gap, solvable with a clearer rule or a better spreadsheet. Often, it isn't. The gap is frequently psychological — a mechanism running beneath conscious awareness, doing its work regardless of how much the person consciously understands about diversification, risk, or the mathematics of a winning streak. A reader can know, with total intellectual clarity, that a single lucky trade proves very little about their own skill, and still feel the identical settled certainty this book has spent its length describing the next time an ambiguous bet happens to pay off. Closing that gap between knowing and feeling isn't a matter of more information. It's a matter of naming the mechanism precisely enough, and often enough, that it becomes possible to catch in the moment it's actually operating — which is the entire task this book, and every book in this library, sets out to do.

If a specific chapter in this book landed harder than the others, that's worth paying attention to on its own terms, not as a verdict on your character but as useful information about which specific door your own next overconfident bet is most likely to walk through. Keep that chapter in mind. The pattern it describes will very likely be the one that shows up again, in some new disguise, the next time a genuinely ambiguous result goes your way — and having already seen it named and explained once is most of what it takes to recognize it the second time, before the story it's telling you gets a chance to finish writing itself.

If this book helped you catch the shape of your own story a little sooner than you would have otherwise, the next useful step is simple: notice it again, next time, before it finishes writing itself. That's the whole practice. It doesn't get more complicated than that, and it doesn't need to.

A final word on the specific pattern this volume covers, since it's worth saying once more, plainly, before these pages close. Winning is not the problem. Wanting to feel proud of a good call is not the problem. The problem is narrower, and considerably more fixable, than either of those things: it's the quiet, automatic conversion of a favorable, ambiguous outcome into a settled belief about your own durable skill, made without ever pausing to ask how much of the outcome the world actually handed you for free. Ask that question honestly, often enough, and the rest of what this book describes loses most of its grip. That's not a small thing to walk away with. For a pattern this expensive, it may be one of the more valuable habits a reader can build from any single book in this entire library.

Also in the Series

Every book in The Money Instinct library stands on its own — read them in any order. If this one was useful, the library continues:

The Money Instinct

The Secrecy Instinct

The Underearning Instinct

The Shame Instinct

The Panic Instinct

The Merge Instinct

The Ceiling Instinct

The Windfall Instinct

The Control Instinct

The Legacy Instinct

The Comparison Instinct

The Enabling Instinct

The Austerity Instinct

The Paralysis Instinct

The Retirement Instinct

The Divorce Instinct

The Enough Instinct

The Vigilance Instinct

The Generosity Instinct